Praise for *Building*

"You would do well to embrace the many truths of this book on how being ~~~~~~ nt leads to making a significant impact.
—Gene Pickelman, President and CEO, Tri-Star Trust Bank

"...broad with relatable real-life examples of both business and everyday life matters."
—Raymond K. Stephens, Employee and Labor Relations Consultant, Dow

"...provides a clear roadmap on how to build a business the right way. This is a must-read.
—Henry Reyna, President, Secure Solutions LLC

"Very accessible and easy to understand, the stories and case studies bring the points home powerfully and in tangible ways."
—So-Young Kang, Founder and Chief Energizer, Gnowbe, Singapore

"...skillfully and refreshingly guides the reader in the "how-to's" of designing, building, and sustaining mission-minded, values-driven and mutually caring work environments today."
—John "Barney" Barnes, Commander US Navy

"...is this century's handbook for people who sincerely want to make a positive difference in their lives, their workplace, their community, and the world."
—Rhonda Sciortino, Chairperson of Successful Survivors Foundation

"The insights in this book are spot on."
—Ken Horn, former Michigan State Senator

"...provides direct and targeted ideas for developing a strong foundation that will serve any organization or effort, big or small."
—Beth Charlton, BSN RN, MHA, President/CEO, Covenant HealthCare

"...gives leaders an easy-to-read 'roadmap' that will enhance their business/organizational effectiveness towards optimal success."
—Trevor Knoesen, Founder and CEO, Productivity Improvement Consulting

"...contains powerful tools to help build resilient teams. It can help all organizations to grow and create life-giving teams."

—**Ric Olson,** President, Gantec Inc.

"...uses a clear, concise approach punctuated by real life examples outlining a road-map to success for any organization wanting to reach the next level."

—**John Kosanovich,** Executive Vice President and CEO of Covenant Medical Group

"...brings new content centered around the root issue behind building an effective and lasting team culture—resiliency."

—**Barry Robinson,** Vice President of Business Development, Util Auditors

"...useful information on practical leadership skills that will benefit leaders at any level and in any industry."

—**Ed Bruff,** former CEO, Covenant HealthCare

"...provides a detailed step-by-step process on how resiliency and perseverance can establish a synergistic team that values long term trust and commitment."

—**Marilyn Skrocki JD, MBA,** Professor Health Sciences, Saginaw Valley State University

"...an exceptional asset to aid leaders in growing and maintaining successful relation-ships through resiliency."

—**Maher Ghanem, MD,** Associate Professor of General Surgery, CMU College of Medicine

"I'm going to recommend this book for organizations both large and small, for profits and nonprofits because this book is a rare one-size-fits-all application."

—**Jimmy E. Greene,** CEO and President, Associated Builders and Contractors

"...gives practical tools and reminds us that all great teams are resilient! Phenomenal!"

—**Brian Pruitt,** All-American Football Player, Central Michigan University

"...condenses extremely powerful strategies and insights that have proven effective for those who take them to heart and properly apply, and apply, and apply..."

—**Andrew Jonathan Forester,** Lifetime Entrepreneur

"...gives us valuable keys to bring our businesses to fruition."

—**Fr. Ludovic Bard,** Vicar, St. Vincent de Paul

BUILDING RESILIENT TEAMS

**Transform Your Workplace,
Your Community & Your World**

BRIAN D. MOLITOR

BUILDING RESILIENT TEAMS

Text Copyright © 2023 Brian D. Molitor

Library of Congress Cataloging-in-Publication

Data is available upon request.

ISBN: 978-1-57826-940-2

Printed in the United States

10 9 8 7 6 5 4 3 2 1

DEDICATION

I dedicate this book to all of the overcomers who get knocked down but refuse to stay down. I salute...

- The combat veteran returning from foreign soil.
- The single parent fighting to make the best future for the children.
- The ones working at entry-level jobs they never wanted, so they can become what they always wanted to become.
- The bullied child that never quits.
- Countless others. You know who you are.

I want you to know that you are not alone, your suffering is not in vain, and your future is much brighter than you can imagine.

You may not know it, but those around you see you and are proud of your willingness to fight, to heal, and to succeed. Your resilience is inspiring, encouraging, and gives us hope for ourselves.

Well done, good and faithful ones... well done.

CONTENTS

CONTENTS

PREFACE

Years ago, while leading a teambuilding session in Kentucky, I met a man who modeled the concepts of resiliency that are the focus of this book. His name was Tran, a diminutive middle-aged man of Vietnamese descent that served as a department manager. His staff saw him as caring, kind, professional, and they noted that his trademark smile rarely left his face.

During one of the breaks in the seminar, I got to spend some one-on-one time with Tran, so I asked about his story... here is what I heard.

South Vietnam had been home to many generations of his ancestors, and he loved his nation. In the early 1960s, he moved his wife and three young children to the capital city of Saigon to take an executive position with one of the many government agencies headquartered there. For more than a decade, he and his family enjoyed full lives, despite the war that was being fought mostly in the northern part of their nation. Saigon was safe, so the children went to school, enjoying classmates, and growing into healthy teenagers.

However, in the early 1970s, the war that was once so far away crept closer to Saigon as enemy troops moved swiftly south. On April 30th, 1975, the city of Saigon fell. Many that had supported the government and their families were targeted by the opposing forces and panic swept the city. Some citizens escaped, but many could not. Tran did his best to lead his family to safety, but they became separated, and his wife and children were killed. Tran's only option was to run to the end of a long pier that extended into the South China sea. With certain death behind him, Tran jumped into the water, intending to swim rather than be killed by the swarming troops.

Miraculously, a departing ship picked up the exhausted man and after several weeks, brought him to America as a refugee. Tran arrived with the shirt on his back, no identification, no proof of his advanced degrees or work experience, no connections, and burdened with the knowledge that his beloved wife and children had lost their lives.

While many might have fallen into despair, Tran chose another path. He enrolled in college and received the first of two degrees earned in this nation. Soon, he was hired by a company that started him near the bottom, but realizing his wisdom and potential, quickly promoted him to a management position. While there, he met a wonderful woman, was married, bought a house, and began his life once again.

As Tran told his story, I found myself with tears in my eyes and deep admiration for this wonderful human being who had lost all, yet because he possessed the profound qualities of faith, hope, and resilience, he pressed on to recreate a beautiful life.

Like Tran, we have all been created with an amazing ability to overcome challenges, adversity, and chaos. Since we live much of our lives in the context of teams and organizations, we can bring that same type of faith, hope, and resilience to them all. It is worth the work; it is worth whatever it takes to succeed.

Never give up.

Never give in.

Always believe.

INTRODUCTION

I t is my pleasure to share my nearly forty years of experience building resilient teams and helping leaders grow both personally and professionally.

Holding nothing back, this book shows you a practical, proven way to build excellence and resiliency into your team, whether you are part of an innovative startup company or an existing organization that has been around for decades.

If you follow the steps as outlined, chances are exceptionally good that you will succeed, and many lives will be changed for the better. If you get weary or if doubts creep in, be sure to read over the Success Stories of Resilient Teams that you will find throughout the book. These are short interviews with leaders who have been where you are today. They share the good, bad, and ugly of organizational life and what it took to resiliently respond to challenges without giving up.

Please know that a cornerstone of my work throughout the world has been taking complex concepts and processes and making them simple ... that is what you will find on the pages that follow. A simple approach to team excellence and resilience to carry you through any challenge you may face in the future.

I encourage you to dream dreams so big that they scare you ... just a bit; to bless others along the way, and above all, to enjoy the journey.

CHAPTER 1

THE RESILIENT TEAM

When you hear the word "team," what comes to mind? Do you picture the long-range shooting Golden State Warriors of the NBA or perhaps a bunch of neighborhood kids playing softball in a nearby park? Maybe your mind's eye sees a group of executives gathered around a huge oaken desk or several staff members casually meeting at a neighborhood coffee shop. Our world is made up of teams of all configurations, large and small, and in every realm of life. Some of these teams succeed and others fail due to many factors, but one of the most overlooked keys to success is *resilience*.

Here is why. Every team and every organization faces crises, challenges, and changes that threaten to squelch its purpose, slow its progress, or destroy it altogether. When, not if, challenges come, it is a team's ability to recover rapidly that determines whether it survives and prospers or joins the list of those that have fallen by the wayside.

As you read through this book, keep in mind that terms such as "team" and "organization" are used interchangeably. You may be a seasoned executive of a multinational corporation hoping to reenergize thousands of staff members or you may be a budding entrepreneur about to launch your first company in a corner of your garage.

What makes the need for the marvelous quality of *resilience* even greater is the fact that teams are comprised of individuals, and those individuals are also subject to crises, challenges, and unexpected changes. This combining of factors creates some exciting times for those in leadership. They must successfully guide the team through everything from new regulations, political uncertainties, increased competition, customer demands, working remotely, along with a pandemic or two tossed in for good measure.

Simultaneously, the leaders must have enough time and energy left to provide support for team members who may be wrestling with their own performance-crippling issues such as broken relationships, health problems, financial pressures, and more. Given these challenges, how can any team expect to survive, let alone succeed? In a word... *resilience.*

A *resilient team* is one that experiences a crisis, challenge, or change and then quickly returns to or exceeds pre-crisis levels of performance. Exactly how does resilience work? How is it infused into a team? What is the secret that causes one team to bounce back from adversity and another to crumble?

After nearly forty years studying the performance of successful teams and the individuals that lead them, I discovered several distinctive aspects about resilient teams. Here they are.

Resilient teams:

1. Anticipate future challenges and proactively develop strategies to address them.

2. Are steadfast in Mission, Values and Culture, but flexible in methods, adjusting as needed to continue to perform at high levels.

3. Prepare team members with education, training, and mentoring to overcome adversity and insure consistency of performance.

4. Team leaders trust their organization's culture in the midst of the storm and never panic.

5. Team leaders remain connected to team members, understanding their concerns, hopes, and skills.

Notice that the majority of the concepts above are applied *before* a crisis hits ... not during. If you fail to properly prepare your team, the only thing that develops during troubling times are migraines and mistakes. We can do better.

This prework for resilience includes having an unshakable culture built upon a clear mission and values, having leaders that are linked and aligned around clear expectations, having staff members that are skilled in their work, and having positive attitudes throughout the team. Here is the great news ... regardless of the challenges your team will face, there is a step-by-step process to get you where you want to go. By following the steps, your business can prosper, your nonprofit can successfully serve your clients, and your family can flourish. The process is relatively simple, however, there are some complexities and subtleties that must be understood to make your journey easier...and less stressful. Regardless of which type of team you are on, the basic elements and steps in the process are the same.

The Process of Growth and Transformation

Here are the six basic elements involved in building resilience into a new organization or instilling resilience into an existing one:

- Establishing your foundation
- Determining your purpose and direction
- Organizing your work
- Creating your culture
- Preparing your people
- Leaving your legacy

It is particularly important to note that these elements are sequential and must be approached in that way. This is not a menu where you select a couple of things and forget the rest. Each element builds on the one before it so skipping steps will leave you stumbling and likely starting over.

As you embark on this marvelous journey of creating or recreating your team, embrace the fact that resistance, problems, and challenges are simply part of the process. Your team's resiliency ensures that the journey will continue.

CHAPTER 2

UNLEASHING THE POWER OF AGREEMENT

Fact #1: Every team has a culture.

Fact #2: A positive culture increases resiliency and likelihood of success, a negative culture lowers resiliency and the likelihood of success.

Fact #3: If a team's culture is positive, it happened by design; if a team's culture is negative, it happened by default.

Shaping Your Team's Culture

The modern concept of culture comes from the centuries-old Latin word, *cultura*, which means *growing* or *tending*. It refers to cultivating soil in preparation for planting crops. This description provides a great image as we think about our own teams or organizations. Gardens and fields that have been carefully tended, prepared, and cultivated stand the best chance of growing healthy crops. In like manner, gardens and fields that are largely ignored also produce crops in abundance . . . however, the crops are worthless weeds.

Of course, within organizations, we are not growing plants, but rather people. So, the "tending" happens through the development of productive relationships, opening lines of communication, aligning vision, values, and other activities.

The Not-So-Secret Ingredient for a Positive Culture

British statesman Sir Winston Churchill, King David of ancient Israel, American president Abraham

Lincoln, civil rights champion Martin Luther King, Jr., Jesus Christ of Nazareth, and Mahatma Gandhi seem very different, however, they had much in common. Each had a vision, accepted their missions, lived by sets of values, faced significant challenges, built successful teams, showed tenacious resiliency, and their efforts brought about massive transformation in the culture around them. But how did they do it? Power of personality? Fiery speeches? Right place at the right time? Those things helped, but there was something more.

The not-so-secret ingredient in building resilient teams is what I refer to as the *Power of Agreement*. Here is how and why it works. There are many sources of natural power in the world today including wood, coal, electricity, gasoline, nuclear, and solar. Each has distinct qualities, however, there a unique power that is unleashed when two or more people commit to a vision or course of action. Once this initial agreement occurs, they begin sharing ideas, motivating each other, jointly solving problems, and implementing strategies for transformation. This is true in marriage, in professional sports, in the marketplace, and in countless other team-oriented situations.

Another word for this phenomenon is one that has been around for decades, *synergy*. This simply means that the combined results of two or more people working together are superior to the results produced if they worked separately. Sounds like smoke and mirrors, right? It is not.

The old saying, two heads are better than one, helps us better understand the concept, but there is more to it. Under the proper circumstances, this dynamic multiplication of output is not just a sharing of what is in one's head. Instead, it occurs on a deeper level, in the heart. This occurs when two or more people are mentally and emotionally committed to a vision or mission, and then they work sacrificially to overcome any challenge, resiliently bounce back from adversity, and fully seize the opportunity. Organizations that harness this *Power of Agreement* are in a position to achieve superior results.

Most Valuable Assets

See if you agree with the following phrase that has made its way into countless corporate statements of purpose . . . People are our Most Valuable Assets. If you agreed, I invite you to think again. In reality, it is only **the *right* people that are your most valuable assets**. All too often, leaders try to achieve success with the wrong people in key positions, which results in frustration and failure for all involved. Of course, you need a host of other things such as capital, buildings, supplies, equipment, technology, information, etc. however, without the right people working together, your quest for success will either fail or fall short of its potential.

We should always be looking for new technology to assist us in our quest for excellence, but remember that robots, kiosks, and computers can never replace the need for human beings to be integrally involved in your organization. Why? Because electronic gadgets cannot think, feel, or sincerely react to the needs of individuals; nor can they create or innovate. We have all experienced the frustration of calling a customer service "help" line only to be stuck with a mindless robo-helper that never quite helps. Most prefer to speak to a real person about our real problems.

Whether your team is a multi-national company, a trendy boutique, or a corner coffee shop, remember that human beings have been divinely equipped to create, innovate, and overcome seemingly insurmountable obstacles. We are resilient and in the right environment, can stage Rocky-like comebacks time and time again.

The Power of Ownership

There is a second "power" that you need to unleash within your team. That is the power of ownership. During public training seminars, I often ask the attendees what initially seems like a silly a question: *How many of you wash a rental car before returning it?* In several decades, only one person ever raised his hand. Thousands of others explained that they do not wash rental cars because *they do not own them.* In other words, they need transportation, so they pay a set amount of money for the use of a vehicle, but their concern and commitment end there. Leaders that fail to comprehend the power of ownership sentence themselves to months of hard labor when attempting to implement even the simplest change.

Ownership is not a matter of stock percentages or formal partnerships. Instead, ownership comes when people are allowed input into a team's operation, are respected by their leaders, and can contribute in various ways beyond just the work of their hands. If you fail to involve the people that accompany you on the journey, they will not view the organization as their own and will not bother "washing it." For successful change, involve others early and often. Then, their levels of commitment and resiliency are high, and the odds of succeeding improve greatly.

The Opportunity

Michelangelo was once asked how he created such beautiful sculptures out of shapeless blocks of granite. He humbly replied that the beauty was always hidden within the stone—he simply removed the parts that hid the beauty.

I can only imagine how many times the artist stuck the chisel before seeing his vision come to life. Chances are good that he had days when he became weary, when the stone refused to cooperate, when self-doubts crept in and yet, he never quit. His resilience sustained him and left the world a more beautiful place.

You and I have similar opportunities in our professional and personal lives.

We live within the context of multiple "teams" that require dedicated work to maintain them properly.

Each is composed of people interacting with others for a multitude of reasons. Each has a "culture" based on its mission,—values, and relationships that develop either by design or by default. Each faces challenges, problems and existential threats that have the potential to leave the mission muddled, the values compromised, and relationships broken.

When, not if, these problems come, it is not time to bury our heads or throw up our hands in surrender. There is a better way. We can seize the opportunity to roll up our sleeves, release our resilience, and begin the process of positive change. Like Michelangelo, we can work to uncover the beauty that lies dormant within our teams and within ourselves.

SUCCESS STORY:
GANTEC, INC.

An interview with Ric Olson, co-founder and President of Gantec, Inc.

G antec, Inc. was founded in 2005, by Ric Olson and three other partners in Midland, Michigan. The vision was to create partnerships with villages in Africa, purchase natural materials for import back to America, and use those natural materials to produce innovative technologies for the developed world's agriculture sector.

Gantec, Inc. pursues a triple bottom line of economic opportunity, environmental improvement, and community development. Working with universities and independent laboratories, Gantec, Inc.'s products have been proven to enhance plant growth in fruit trees, berries, and vegetables of all sorts. In addition, their technology makes it possible to see enhanced growth in plants without excessive use of chemical pesticides, herbicides, and other substances thereby protecting our environment. President Olson has made many trips to African countries such as Mauritania and Senegal, traveled to remote villages to meet with elders, and built strong relationships thereby securing an endless supply of natural materials that are then shipped to the United States for processing. By purchasing natural materials from the villages, Gantec Inc. creates sustainable jobs for many, especially women and children, that otherwise would have no means of support.

The Gantec, Inc. vision is to create value for *all* involved, and never to exploit people or resources as they deliver innovation and genuine value to employees, customers, and communities around the world.

Question: What were your greatest challenges?

Ric: We have amazing innovative technology, but the market is slow to accept new ideas, even when the old ways are poisoning the earth and doing harm to the owners of greenhouses, farmers, and their employees and family members since many growers are part of multi-generational businesses. So, our challenge was slow acceptance of a new way of doing things and it was difficult to always have the working capital we needed.

Also, at times, it was hard to focus our energies because our technology could be used in so many different markets and products. It took time to know where to concentrate our efforts, but thankfully we are now hitting our stride.

Question: When times got tough, how did the concept of resilience play a part in your continued success?

Ric: Staying focused on what was right in front of us really helped. Praying for wisdom did as well.

Question: What are you most proud of?

Ric: The countless people who helped move us along and the sacrifices made by many to bring us to where we are today. Also, that we have developed a unique technology that helps people, plants, and our environment.

Question: Was there a time when your team needed to be revised, transformed, or rebuilt?

Ric: Yes, we originally focused on a single natural product, Neem, sourced from a single African country, Mauritania. Over time, we branched out and procured many other natural ingredients from around the globe. When this happened, we had world-class scientists join the company to develop technology to extract the bio-chemistry from the natural plants and seeds in a sustainable fashion. We looked at applications for the materials first in the flower sector but soon moved our focus to the North American agricultural sector. We began as a research and development company, then transitioned to a production company, and then became more of a technology company that helps solve grower challenges using organic methods and products.

Question: Have you done any training, development, or coaching for your leaders or staff? If so, what did you do and what was the impact?

Ric: We have used StrengthsFinder for all our employees. We have regular staff meetings which begin with prayer and offer thanksgiving for the blessings in each of our lives. We have encouraged taking classes to build solid foundations for all our employees. We also train our staff in the complex technology needed to formulate our products. Some of our staff are world-class scientists and some are workers who recently were released from incarceration. We all work together as a team, giving and receiving respect.

Question: What advice do you have for anyone wanting to either launch a new organization or to revitalize an existing one?

Ric: Find your *Why* ... in other words, decide if you are in it to make money, to change the world, to develop people, or for some other reason. Tough times will come and if you are not clear on why you are putting in the effort, then you may be tempted to give up.

Also, build a team of like-minded people. When you grow and add staff, be a servant leader that leads by example. Listen, listen, love, love. Take care of your staff and customers and they will take care of you.

CHAPTER 3

ROADBLOCKS TO RESILIENCE

You and your team members are bound to run into a few roadblocks on the journey. If you are launching a new organization, your roadblocks may be a lack of finances, staff, space, logistics and more. For those of you looking to transform an existing organization, the roadblocks often come in the form of resistance to trying something different because "that's how it has always been done in the past." Don't believe me? Try implementing a "simple" change in how things are done and watch how quickly the nay-sayers and boo-birds sound off. The good news is that once you know what to watch for, you can spot the roadblocks from miles away and develop strategies to go over, under, around or through them. The following are common roadblocks that hinder efforts to launch or grow organizations. Not only do they slow the rate of progress a team can make, but they also damage or destroy the team's resilience.

Roadblock #1: Natural Resistance to Change

Mark Twain once said that the only person that enjoys change is a baby with a wet diaper. The rest of us become comfortable with life's routines and tend to resist, run from, or challenge any change that is not obviously in our best interest. Why? Because change brings with it many unknowns, and fear of the unknown often has a paralyzing effect. People stay at jobs that barely supply enough income to meet their needs because they fear leaving the security of the known. As bizarre as it seems, some stay in abusive relationships for the same reason; predictable misery seems better than the uncertainties of change.

Another cause of the resistance is a lack of trust. At one time or another, we have all been lied to, deceived, and/or taken advantage of and while we may forgive such acts, it is hard to forget them. When a break of trust happens within a team, department, or entire organization, then credibility is lost, commitment drops, and people shift into a "wait and see" mode of operation. Once bitten, twice shy. Twice bitten... forget about it! Trust broken, at any level, takes time to rebuild. It is possible to do so, but until it happens, resistance to change will continue to hinder progress.

Roadblock #2: Past Failures

"We tried that before and it didn't work." This is a common response to a proposed change. What the doubters overlook is that although the statement may be true, it fails to recognize one of the greatest qualities of humanity: We have an innate ability to learn, grow, and change.

Today, we can analyze yesterday's defeats and turn them into tomorrow's victories. The spouse who sincerely desires a healthy marriage after several failed attempts may well succeed. Why? Because the pain of loneliness and heartache demands another try. Priorities have changed and "family" has taken on new importance. Wise counselors, books about marriage, and simple reflection on past missteps combine to forge a new level of commitment. Personal pain is an unpleasant teacher, but an effective one.

As leaders, we must free ourselves from the shackles of past mistakes and failed attempts if we are going to change our little part of the world. In one sense, we need to become young again, to rekindle the wonderful quality of faith in things that we cannot see. It is not as hard as it sounds. In fact, we have done it for years. As little children, the first time we tried to walk, we fell. How did we react? Did we give up? Were we content to crawl for the rest of our lives just because our first attempts failed? Of course not. Instead, we recognized that there was a new world waiting to be discovered, so we got up and tried again until we succeeded.

Roadblock #3: Fear of Power Loss

It is a rare person that does not enjoy some amount of power, position, authority, and/or the perks that go with them. Once we have power of any sort, it is often hard to let it go.

I witnessed this firsthand years ago when consulting with one of the Big Three automotive manufacturers in my home state of Michigan. At the time, there were thousands of union workers, laboring in scores of manufacturing plants and foundries in the area. Business was booming, but the union and management groups were always at odds, showing little interest in working together. Instead, the high-level leaders of each side spent much of their time threatening strikes and lockouts while maneuvering for an advantage in future contract negotiations. At the shop floor levels, individual supervisors and union members waged constant battles, punctuated by disciplinary "write up's" and the obligatory filing of grievances. A mess for sure, but when people were buying vehicles and the money is rolling in . . . who cares, right?

At least a few insightful individuals saw the storm brewing and pushed for more amenable relations. As a result, I was asked to meet with top leaders of both sides and after many long discussions about the power of agreement, I gave them a strategy of respectful cooperation that would allow them to retain their identities and authority yet begin to function more as partners instead of adversaries.

Some leaders listened and tried; others laughed at the notion of "cooperation" and continued the power-based infighting. Some locations implemented the plan, but many did not. The reason? They saw no need for change and surely did not want to give up any power. Sadly, predictably, things began to change ... for the worse. Foreign manufacturers cracked the quality code and began producing excellent vehicles at competitive prices. Changes in international treaties, tariffs, and trade agreements made it possible for the manufacturers to literally move entire product lines from Michigan to Mexico not only for cheaper labor but also for more predictable, cooperative relationships.

In those same areas of Michigan today, there remain only a few automotive plants and union jobs have dwindled to a tiny fraction of what they once were. How sad. It was not fate that brought about the decline. Instead, it was the failure on the part of leaders to build productive relationships, open lines of honest communication, and to be willing to give up some "power" for the good of all.

Roadblock #4: Conflicting Programs, Policies, and Activities

Every organizational change automatically upsets the status quo and moves somebody's "cheese". This means that at least some existing program, policy, project, personnel, or activity will be postponed, eliminated, or added to when a change is implemented. Also, because of limitations on budgets, personnel, space, and/or time, there is always competition [either healthy or unhealthy] for resources. This is especially true for startups when every moment, dollar, and/or inch of space is precious. Change often means a reallocation of resources, which can send shockwaves of anxiety throughout the organization.

Your measures of success, such as productivity, quality, safety, customer service, employee engagement, and profitability, are often in competition with each other. Money, time, space, and other resources invested in one area means they will not be spent in another. Faster productivity may cause lower quality. More demanding customer service may cause lower employee engagement. These conflicts may well lead to hard feelings among staff unless handled with care. Whatever you plan to do "new," means that something "old" must change. Just be ready for it.

This zero-sum conflict is seen in many areas of life. For example, my wife and I raised four healthy active children and during the school years, it was a battle to establish and maintain priorities. For several years, I confess that we did a terrible job of it. Between school activities, sports, spending quality time together, getting "in shape," we ran ourselves ragged. Can you relate? Eventually, we realized that we were trying to do too much with too few resources and that many of our goals were in direct conflict. It took many family meetings before we finally resolved the conflicts, set new priorities, and a sense of order was restored to our home.

Roadblock #5: Lack of Patience

Much of our society is in a hurry. We expect fast food, self-checkout lanes, and internet speeds that are quicker than lightning strikes. Television commercials have been reduced to just a few seconds for fear of the audience losing interest. Of course, there is no longer a need to drive to a store when with just a few mouse clicks, Mr. Bezos' crew, and a host of newcomers, will deliver countless products to your front door.

Naturally, the instant gratification craze does not stop there. According to the Consumer Credit Review, in 2022, the average American holds $6200 in credit card debt. We gladly use cards to get what we want now and pay for it later, accepting, perhaps as a form of penance, the high rate of interest added to the bill each month.

Impatience has become part of our very souls, often with painful consequences. When I go to restaurants, I hate waiting for soup to cool... It just takes too long. I think that the cooks see me coming and turn their scalding cauldrons up another hundred degrees or so. Once served, I typically wait no more than fifteen seconds and then dig in despite the steam swirling off the surface of the bowl. The result? A severely burned tongue, which causes more delay than if I had waited longer in the first place.

Just know that anyone you enlist to help with your vision of positive change will likely be afflicted by the 'hurry-up' paradigm, so set proper timelines and expectations to avoid getting burned.

Roadblock #6: Dysfunctional Interpersonal Relationships

Regardless of which goods or services you provide, your organization is in the business of relationships. The way in which your people act and interact internally and externally, impacts its resiliency and largely determines the team's ultimate success or failure. When team members work well together, it produces open communication, trust-based relationships, productive approaches to conflict resolution, joint problem solving and decision-making, and a host of other positive outcomes. When they either do not work well together or in the worst case, work against each other, the results are completely opposite. Communication shuts down, trust is lost, conflicts go unresolved, problems are left to fester, and decisions are delayed.

This is a real showstopper when it comes to organizational change and the pursuit of excellence at any level. Interpersonal relationships must be strong enough to withstand the strain of change. Teams that overlook this fact often try a wide variety of programs to enhance performance, but sadly, they just do not work.

Roadblock #7: Lack of Leadership Commitment

I saved the best . . . or worst, for last. The lack of commitment on the part of team leaders is the most difficult roadblock to overcome. The support of leaders, because of their positional power is vital, especially in the early stages of the change process. During this period, leaders initiate most of the action and keep the process moving forward by their investment of time, money, support, counsel, and other resources.

I once was invited to help build resilience in an organization that manufactured various automotive parts from sheet metal. The general manager proudly told me about his regular lectures to the workforce about the importance of productivity, quality, safety, and team spirit. Despite his use of the latest buzz words, his employees remained uninspired and decidedly *un*-resilient. A quick tour of the plant revealed the reason for their indifference. The machines, incredibly loud and virtually impossible to adjust for fine quality improvement, were relics from the 1940s. At unpredictable intervals, these mechanical volcanoes spewed hot oil onto unsuspecting employees below. In addition, the plant had no automated system for handling materials, which meant that employees had to physically carry each piece of razor-sharp metal from one machine to the next. It was easy to identify the most senior staff by the number of scars on their hands and arms.

The impact of this work environment on the company's bottom-line was predictable. It suffered low productivity, poor quality, and abysmal profitability. Further evidence of the chaos was seen in high rates of absenteeism, employee turnover, grievances, and injuries. Customer complaints were common since error and rework delayed most product deliveries. This was a perfect location for a cultural change process and with support from top management, the employees were ready to make great things happen.

Unfortunately, the plant manager's commitment to change was not there. Instead of apologizing for allowing the company to fall into disrepair, he gave heated lectures to employees on the need for *them* to build quality into *their* products. The manager scolded *them* for *their* lack of productivity and threatened *them* with job loss if *they* did not improve. All the while, he refused to invest the funds necessary to upgrade the machinery, provide safety equipment, and clean up the plant. Epic fail...

The Road Map

Now that we have identified potential roadblocks to watch out for, it is time to create strategies to get around them on the way to our destination. None of them are insurmountable, but any have the potential to slow or even stop progress for the team. So, grab the GPS, punch in the coordinates, and let's find the best way forward.

CHAPTER 4

GETTING PAST THE ROADBLOCKS

W hile there is a temptation to take a "quick fix"
approach to team success, it is much better to
take a bit more time to employ proven foundational principles. Here are three keys that help get past
the roadblocks.

Foundation #1:
Long-Term Commitment

Commitment is an extremely powerful force in any professional or personal context. Consider a wedding ceremony when two people make life-long commitments to each other. Those pledges are not made to sustain the relationship during the honeymoon ... that is the easy part. Instead, the vows are for times of testing and trials that come after the honeymoon ends. Approached in this way, a marriage is a life-long journey, not a one-year contract with renewable options.

This same level of commitment is needed for organizational growth and transformation. Without commitment to a long-term process, efforts to grow will falter. At the first sign of trouble, some will opt for returning to the "good old days," Forgetting that if the old days had been so *good*, the change would not have been initiated in the first place. Without a long-term commitment to transformation, there can be no resilience.

Foundation #2: High Levels of Involvement from Others

Organizational development requires support from all levels if it is to succeed. Years ago, I first shared the following *Molitorism* to help clients remember this important truth.

Meaningful Involvement = Support and Commitment

In other words, if you want your ideas to be embraced and supported by others, then you must involve them in the strategic planning process *before* all the final decisions are made. The reason for the high level of involvement is simple, yet compelling. People support and commit to things that they help create. Remember, people do not wash rental vehicles for one fundamental reason: They do not own them.

This is much more than an attempt by leaders to be "nice." It is a precise strategy for enhanced performance, stronger employee engagement, and increased competitiveness. As with many aspects of organizational development, there are some subtleties that must be understood. Involvement has its limits. For example, leaders do not ask staff to write the mission statement, establish core strategies, or decide on high-level financial or market-driven decisions. Instead, staff members are invited to give input on decisions that directly involve them and their work because in those realms, they are the experts. Involved team members are more resilient, more committed to the transformation process, and are willing to sacrifice to see the mission accomplished.

Foundation #3: High-Quality Relationships

Positive change and team improvement cannot be dictated, mandated, or forced upon people. It must be presented in a way that creates a desire for change in the hearts of those impacted. Positive change occurs most rapidly and efficiently in an atmosphere of trust, openness, and supportive relationships.

Mature leaders realize that they cannot do it all by themselves, despite society's constant barrage of messages to the contrary. Through the years, popular songs have captured the world's self-centered approach to life and success. Musical hits like *I Did It My Way* and *I Gotta Be Me* may be entertaining, but they are not accurate. In this life, little happens without the support of others.

I am not saying that we must create some sort of bizarre corporate brotherhood where employees hold hands and sing the company song to get motivated for work every morning. However, I *am* saying that interpersonal relationships, teamwork, and mutual respect play an immense role in the team's ability to manage change and to bounce back following times of great challenge.

For nearly forty years, I have studied a wide variety of organizations to determine what causes them to either prosper or fail. Amazingly, the primary cause of low organizational effectiveness is not a lack of funds, outdated equipment, or anything else related to the nuts and bolts of its operation. Instead, the primary obstacle to success was, is, and will be a negative culture as evidenced by **poor interpersonal relationships** within the organization itself. This is not the absence of "niceness," but rather a lack of respect, trust, communication, cooperation, and commitment to the cause. This always begins at the top . . .

In today's world, leaders and owners often have a stronger relationship with their work than with their workers. It is common for managers, supervisors, and administrators to know what their followers *do,* but little about who they *are.* Not surprisingly, followers know even less about their leaders. In these impersonal settings, it becomes an "everyone for themselves" environment which leads to a myriad of problems. Conversely, in organizations where productive relationships are created, valued, and nurtured, the mindset is more Musketeer-like "all for one and one for all." Resiliency is a natural outcome in such environments.

Once the relationships are built, the actual work itself can be accomplished with much greater efficiency and, believe it or not . . . enjoyment, and that is the way it is supposed to be.

NATIONAL NAIL CORPORATION

An interview with Scott Baker, CEO and Chairman of National Nail Corporation

Many years ago, National Nail Corp. was formed in Grand Rapids, Michigan, by two friends with the grand vision of making screen doors from used apple crates. Since then, the company has evolved significantly as it began making and selling a wide variety of fastening equipment.

Its current CEO and Chairman, Scott Baker, and his team have taken the company to a whole new level. They added other locations in Syracuse New York, Atlanta Georgia, Houston Texas, Los Angeles California, and Seattle Washington. Also, they have employed more than 3000 people and are the primary customer for mills in Asia that employ thousands of workers. The company now invents new tools that transform parts of the building industry, thereby creating additional employment opportunities.

Scott joined the organization in 1997 and under his leadership and the revisioning process he launched in 2008, during some of the worst economic times since the great depression, the company's value has risen 1000%.

Question: What were your greatest challenges?

Scott: In 1997, there were several. 1) Our culture. The owners were not inclusive. They chose not to invite other key "managers" into the leading of the company. As such, the managers knew little about how the business really worked. 2) Unhealthy relationship between the union and hourly, and salary and office. 3) Lack of vision, and direction for the future. 4) Unclear performance standards for employees. Little accountability. 5) The company was doing reasonably well and did not see the reason for any substantive change.

Today, the challenges include 1) Acquiring talent at the senior levels to keep pace with the growth we have secured and drive future growth. 2) Innovation is moving at a rapid pace whether in product or technology. Significant investments in AI and other analytics toolsets are a must. 3) The increased presence of Private Equity which can be disruptive given their financial "only" motives. 4) We are growing with challenging large customers (THD/Lowes) who demand much of us. 5) The Geopolitical impacts on our global supply chain. 6) In addition to securing talent, we must be better at developing talent. 7) And probably the most significant for the long-term is finding my replacement. The company is very dependent on me to grow our culture and our key customer relationships.

Question: When times got tough, how did the concept of resilience play a part in your continued success?

Scott: I learned to lean more into my friends, scripture, reading books, and journaling. Teaching is a source of energy for me. I try to get more sleep and exercise more as well. As the CEO, many will be watching me and how I respond. Hence, the above is necessary for me.

My mindset is to use the trial for growing me, my team, and anyone I can encounter. Romans 5 is replayed daily in my mind. I believe and have experienced God's love, grace, mercy, and counsel in ways during tough times that I have never "heard" during good times. Tough times are used to test my past development and shape and refine me for the next one.

Question: What are you most proud of?

Scott: A few things. 1) The "it's the right thing to do," servant-focused, faith-based, culture we have developed. Our culture is caring, loving, giving, and growth minded. Many examples of how our culture has impacted our families, customers, communities, suppliers, and our communities. 2) The wealth we have created for our families. More than 10% of our folks have north of $1 million in ESOP for their retirement. This is life changing. Many hourly staff have over $500k. Crazy. 3) We have invented new products, tools, methods that have been industry changing. 4) We have a reputation for being a company that you can trust.

Question: Was there a time when your team needed to be revised, transformed, or rebuilt? Explain.

Scott: Yes. As we grew quickly from 2000–2008, I did not like that we were like many other distributors. We were largely driven by the products of OEM's. Home Depot and Lowes were entering every market, our customers were changing their business models away from DIY, many would fold. Internally, my leadership team was not strong, and had little interest in individual development or growth. The future existence of the company did not look inspiring. I needed to change both our business model and my team. Over the following years, we would establish a leadership brand built around 8 Character traits, exit all OEM brands, and focus on creating our own brands. Good or bad, most of my leadership team would leave or be asked to leave.

Question: Have you done any training, development, or coaching for your leaders or staff? If so, what did you do and what was the impact?

Scott: Regularly. From book clubs, outside speakers/ teachers, annual and quarterly summits, we send folks to outside leadership events, encourage membership in professional associations, and more. We hired a director of training who is bringing even more tools to our folks, and we will be adding another person to this team. We are beginning to engage with outside teachers to further assist me with the development of our folks.

Regarding development, we strive to develop our men and women to be better men and women, husbands and wives, moms, and dads and more. As such, our development does not simply focus on assignment competencies and skillsets.

Question: What advice do you have for anyone wanting to either launch a new organization or to revitalize an existing one?

Scott: Wow. A lot here. The textbook stuff is to have 1) a compelling purpose for doing either; 2) have a shared and compelling vision and 3) the strategies for being able to execute your vision; 4) great people; and 5) the ability to have great execution! Each of these is important; however, the culture built with the people will have the biggest impact on whether the dream is achieved.

But the most important is the belief that you have/ can/bring/do something that is desired by others that you are inspired/called to do. It is this internal belief that will continue to fuel you when it is difficult. It will help get you through the toughest moments and challenge whether you believe it or not. Hebrews 11:1 has been my go-to passage for believing in something I cannot see.

Also, ask yourself what is the motive for starting something new, or for revisioning the organization? How prepared are you and your team for the journey ahead? Do you have a close group of advisors? If not, get one. Do you have a strong team? If not, build one.

CHAPTER 5

A NEW WAY OF LIFE

When seeking positive change and increased resiliency in your team, you have two basic options.

Option #1: Invest in a long-term process that brings a **new way of life** to your team.

Option #2: Implement a **short-term program** and hope for the best.

Let's compare the two options, starting with Option #1: A new way of life. This approach is time-consuming, costly, and since it takes place while existing work is ongoing, it is a bit like riding a bike down a mountain trail . . . while attempting to change the tire at the same time. Sounds challenging, but remember, Option #1 is the surest and most lasting way to transform a team. It is well worth the effort.

As for Option #2, there is one particularly important fact you need to understand about programs . . . they do not last. Much like a television show that opens with fast-paced glimpses of what is to come, then provides a bit of entertainment, and then ends one hour later. No matter how exciting, funny, or touching the program was . . . it is over. And then? It is time for yet another program.

Sadly, in our quest for team success, the pattern is often the same. We launch training *programs*, safety *programs*, diversity *programs*, productivity *programs*, quality *programs*, team building *programs*, and a host of other *programs* that begin with a great deal of fanfare, only to end a short time later. Why? Because the problems that led to the program still exist . . . so we try another short-term solution.

This is especially true in larger organizations where programs regularly pop up in response to problems that someone, somewhere identified. These "new releases" begin with inspired speeches or thunderous threats about the need for improvement. Executives, directors, pastors, and administrators pledge their deep, unending commitment to this new mindset before quietly fading into the background to allow others to make things happen . . . somehow.

The program, often a training program, then begins for all to attend, mandatory, of course. Surely a few hours with a passionate facilitator will transform deeply ingrained thinking about how work is done, right?

Sorry to say, but if the following factors are in place, chances are good that you are implementing programs that will likely fall short of your goals.

1. *May have* high support from top levels of leadership but *does not have* high levels of ownership, involvement, support, and/or commitment from lower-level leaders or team members.

2. Developmental activities are based on the "crisis or problem of the month."

3. Multiple disjointed initiatives are being implemented without clearly defined measures of success.

4. Developmental activities have no clear alignment with the organization's desired culture.

5. Implementation causes confusion, commotion, and chaos rather than simplifying and clarifying issues, thereby reducing the team's resiliency.

Do any of the above look familiar? If so, you likely are involved in running programs, rather than seeking a new way of organizational life.

Lots of Programs, Same Result

Some of the more common programs focus on productivity, quality, and customer service. All good things to be sure. Over time, these programs have been called by many different names including Statistical Process Control, Six Sigma, Quality of Work life, Quality Circles, Employee Engagement, Safety, HRO, and many more. In recent years, many organizations attempted to shape their cultures by employing Toyota's Production System.

All programs have the potential to add complexity, disruption, and confusion, to a workplace that already faces many challenges, but when the new program replaces common words with foreign terms, the challenges can be insurmountable. For example, Toyota's Production System comes with an entirely new vocabulary to explain relatively simple terms. This forces overloaded staff members to learn, pronounce and apply such terms as *RIE, Kaizen, POU, Gemba, TPM, Muri, VOC, VSA, Mura, Muda, Yokoten,* and my personal favorite *Poka-yoke.*

First line supervisors no longer spend time identifying and solving problems. Instead, they now leave their offices to *Gemba,* watching carefully for *Mura, Muda,* or *Muri.* Their untrained eyes attempt to spot opportunities for *Heijunka, Jidoka,* and *Shojinka.* Then, having *Gemba'ed,* they now return [or retreat] to their offices for *Hansei* about *Hoshin Kanri* and if successful, they enter *Yokoten* with other leaders. Confused? So are they. Transforming an organization should make life simpler, not more complex for those who must implement any changes.

With enough initial hype, time, and money thrown at it, any program *may* produce some results as low-hanging fruit and obvious problems are solved. However, as with all programs, it will end. Why? Often, top leaders grow frustrated at the costs, time commitment, and lack of immediate, significant return, so they grab the remote and switch off the program. Here are a few other topics that often become programs within organizations of all types:

- Performance improvement
- Quality
- Safety
- Statistical process control
- Customer service
- LEAN
- Diversity
- Productivity improvement
- Efficiency
- Communication
- Leadership
- Team building
- Problem solving
- Presentation skills

Regardless of what they are called, any of the listed topics *can* make a difference in organizations that are truly ready for them. People can even learn to use foreign terms such as *Gemba* and *Poka-yoke* and apply them properly. However, unless an organization commits to the new philosophy *as a way of life*, then the programs are destined to fail.

Just for Fun

Over time, I have run into some programs that fell way short of the mark.

One company attempted to motivate their struggling leadership group, by bringing in a famous NFL quarterback whose speech was punctuated by the tag line "Throw the Hail Mary." Translated, when things look hopeless, just heave the ball down the field and great things will happen... at least it did for him in one particular game. Of course, motivational speeches cannot fix real problems for a team, so after the costly one-hour presentation, everyone went back to work where nothing had changed. Evidently, the leaders were listening to the speech because for weeks afterward when staff would complain about the same issues that plagued them in the past, the managers would nod knowingly, parrot the phrase "Just throw the Hail Mary" and then walk away.

At one manufacturing plant in Southern Michigan, the management implemented the "Ten Best" suggestion program. The idea was to encourage staff to submit up to ten ideas per year that would improve productivity, quality, or some other aspect of performance. The suggestions had to be turned in by December 15th each year and in response, each staff person that participated would receive a frozen turkey just before Christmas. A few employees took the program seriously and provided written ideas to better the plant throughout the year. However, most staff simply sat down on December 14th, and filled out ten suggestion forms with bizarre ideas, just beating the deadline. Their offerings included such gems as "Cutting holes in the roof to let the hot air out in the summer," followed by "cutting holes in the floor to drain out the water that comes in from the holes in the roof." As promised, just before Christmas, a huge truck pulled up in front of the plant and handed out frozen turkeys to hundreds of snickering staff members.

One of my favorite examples of a program that did not work comes from a small assembly company in Ohio, owned and operated by two brothers. These second-generation leaders had a unique approach to operational transformation that they called "restructuring." Whenever productivity, quality, and/or customer complaint problems reached a certain level, the two would simply switch jobs . . . With loud and proud proclamations to their employees about the exciting changes happening, they would change titles, pack up the contents of their desks, and literally move across the hall into the other's former office.

CHAPTER 6

A NEW VISION FOR YOUR TEAM

"Everything that can be invented has been invented."

That quote comes direct from one Charles Duell, Commissioner for the United States Office of Patents in 1899. Obviously, Mr. Duell was more than a bit short-sighted in his prediction, as innovators still develop new creations each year. This inventing process is the same used to create new teams, organizations, and institutions. Each begins when someone "envisions" something that others have either not yet seen or lacked the commitment to successfully pursue. Regardless of whether the vision is for a new vaccine, the next social media platform, or for turning an abandoned building into a trendy coffee shop, it begins with someone's vision.

This concept of vision is not for the faint of heart or for those that tremble at the thought of change. People that live by the now-famous phrase: *If it ain't broke, don't fix it*, struggle with innovation and transformation. Why? Because to embrace a new vision, you must leave your comfort zones and let go of the old. This is a lot easier than you might think. In fact, we first employed the process when we were children. When asked the universal question "What do you want to be when you grow up?" we instantly declared that we would become firemen, police officers, astronauts, pro-athletes, super-star singers on American Idol, forest rangers, or some other exciting profession. These responses were not well thought-out life plans, but rather the sum of our marvelous daydreams. In our innocence, we pictured a future state of being, using only the power of our imaginations.

There are two basic types of vision when it comes to organizations. First, there is a *creative* vision whereby one or more entrepreneurs imagine the formation of a business, ministry, nonprofit, or other type of company. The second type of vision, *transformative*, is for leaders of existing organizations or teams that must change to reach new levels of performance. In this instance, the imagination is used to picture what is possible, despite the current challenges.

Creative Vision for New Organizations

A creative vision brings a new idea, company, organization, or team to life. There is a precise moment when something that has never been before comes into existence. Often, these ideas happen in response to a problem or opportunity that you experience. No place in town to get a good pizza? Imagine starting your own takeout restaurant. Too many troubled teens with nowhere to go? Picture an innovative youth program, using local church buildings during the week. Can't pay bills on your salary, think about creating a new online business to generate passive income. The possibilities are only limited by our imagination, which the good Mr. Duell certainly underestimated.

Every organization in existence today started as a vision or picture in someone's mind and grew from there. The great inventions of history such as the wheel, electricity, and room service are all innovations born from creative visions. Another powerful example of this concept comes from the 1960s when American President John F. Kennedy shared a compelling vision for the United States' space program: he wanted to put a man on the moon by the end of the decade.

In today's world, we scarcely think about the fact that scores of humans have flown into space, spent time living in orbiting space stations, and have flown back to earth, landing at the place of their choosing. This was certainly not the case when Mr. Kennedy shocked the world with his novel idea. The reaction at the time was predictable . . . Impossible! Fortunately, the president surrounded himself with people that had faith in his dream and the work began. Since nothing like that had ever been done before, there was no existing plan to modify, change, or revise. His amazing project, and the organization to support it, had to be developed from conception to completion. The vision was realized when in 1969, Neil Armstrong walked on the surface of the moon and uttered the now famous words . . . *"one small step for man, one giant leap for mankind."*

Your vision is likely less lofty than the President's, however, it is just as important. Why? Because it is yours. You dreamed it and now you can build it. It all starts with vision.

Transformational Vision for Existing Organizations

The transformational vision most often occurs in an *existing organization* when leaders realize that change is needed for survival. The warning signs often relate to problems with productivity, quality, sales, attendance numbers, employee engagement, and/or others. This realization leads to times of reflection and soul-searching causing leaders to compare the original vision, mission, and values, to the current reality. Has the vision become cloudy? Have they strayed from the path? Have changing conditions blocked the path forcing a significant change of direction? Regardless of what brought about decline, the only way to avoid a premature end to the team is for it to transform.

Vision to Be the Best

Interestingly, a transformative vision may also be cast when an organization is at a high point in its lifecycle. Watchful leaders often identify the existence of significant opportunities for growth, improvement, and/or competitive advantage even during times of great success. We see examples of this transformational mindset in the world of athletics where world-class competitors continually strive to raise their levels of performance. Runners with years of experience and countless trophies still look for ways to outdistance the competition. To do so, they employ innovative approaches of strength training, increased intervals, enhanced nutrition, and computer images of arm and leg movements.

Pioneering leaders around the world envision new product lines, new strategic alliances, and the expansion of existing services into uncharted territory. Enterprising religious leaders find new ways to entice parishioners to spend more time with each other by installing high-tech coffee bars in their lobbies, scheduling times for social gatherings, small group prayer sessions and more.

Transformation can happen almost anywhere...it just takes vision.

How It Is Done

Whether you want to launch a new organization or wish to take an existing one to new heights, the process is essentially the same. Envision, discuss, decide, implement.

I have had the pleasure of helping many entrepreneurs launch new companies. One of my favorites is Gantec Inc. an incredibly innovative biotech company, headquartered in Michigan.

The process I use when facilitating this type of session never changes. I ask members of the group to convert the vision in their minds into words and phrases, and then have them explain both the rationale and even some of the emotion behind the vision. At times, groups dive too deep into details, timelines, structure, and more. When this happens, we step back and return to a discussion about the overarching purpose of the organization. The initial goal is always to have leaders imagine the ultimate destination rather than create a detailed roadmap or long-term strategic plan.

At the first Gantec Inc. planning session, a small group of scientists and I sat around a table, talking about the collective vision which, I confess, seemed impossible. As we talked, the principals envisioned the creation of jobs in African villages, the collection of all-natural plant materials, the shipping of those materials to the USA in huge containers, and ultimately the processing of the materials into organic plant-based products to enhance the growth of valuable fruits, vegetables, and other products. The vision also included new organic products to reduce the use of harmful pesticides, fertilizers, and herbicides across the globe. Like I said, it seemed impossible. But the more the leaders of the group [Dr. Joe Affholter, Dr. Lanny Robbins, Mr. Ric Olson] and I talked, the more possible it seemed. Today, more than ten years after that initial meeting, this amazing company is changing the world of agriculture with its innovative, organic products. It all started with vision.

The creation of a new vision is something to be celebrated, but not for too long before the more challenging work begins. For those wishing to launch a new business, consider the following numbers that are both intoxicating and sobering. According to the Bureau of Labor Statistics, a record breaking 5,400,000 new businesses were launched in the year 2021! That's an amazing statistic, however, so is the fact that on average, more than 20% of those new startups will fail within the first year, and that number rises to more than 50% by year five.

Now, do not get nervous about those numbers, but remember that a vision without a corresponding plan is simply a daydream like we had when we were children. But, when we create a concrete plan to support the vision, we have a good shot at being counted among the successful organizations still making a difference far into the future. We will explore the steps in the planning process in the following chapters.

SUCCESS STORY:
GNOWBE

An interview with So-Young Kang, Founder and CEO of Gnowbe

So-Young Kang launched her company, Gnowbe, with a vision to humanize the world. Their "3C" mission is to raise consciousness, build human connections, and to inspire change.

Gnowbe is a micro-authoring tool for trainers, leaders, coaches and educators to make training more engaging and effective. The name "Gnowbe" stands for "grow knowledge into being" as they are passionate about moving knowledge out of our heads into action which then becomes part of our being. They accomplish their vision by redefining how digital content is created and consumed to be more social, empowering, and impactful. Their approach is through a microlearning, and micro-authoring experience delivered primarily on mobile powered by analytics to provide insights to help people be better.

Gnowbe serves hundreds of organizations across 48 countries from their two main headquarters—San Francisco and Singapore—and with employees across eight countries. They are proud that their global remote team is female led. Gnowbe is a SaaS business whose list of creators and users has more than doubled in the last 12 months.

Question: What were your greatest challenges?

So-Young: Timing and sequencing are always a challenge. As a tech founder who has experience in business before, there is a set of best practices that you want to follow. In a startup, you may not have all the resources you need to execute "best practices" so figuring out what to do and when is difficult. Being able to prioritize, when your team and resources are limited is challenging especially when you know what "great" looks like.

Question: When times got tough, how did the concept of resilience play a part in your continued success?

So-Young: Prayer. Lots of prayer. Good friends to share what's going on and to be emotionally supported. The entrepreneurial journey is tough and is very humbling. It is also important to have a strong support network of colleagues, friends, and advisors to learn from and grow together.

Question: What are you most proud of?

So-Young: I am most proud of the people that have come to share this vision and of the culture we built. We have a passionate, dedicated team of "Gnowbeans" who support each other and do great work. I feel privileged to be able to work with these awesome people. Also, I am proud of the product we built that is now recognized as one of the best microlearning platforms in the world. It gives me joy to know that we improve the lives of so many people.

Question: Was there a time when your team needed to be revised, transformed, or rebuilt? Explain.

So-Young: Always. This is a tech startup, so we are always having to adapt, refine, learn, and relearn. It's a journey of continuous testing, learning, and sharpening. For example, we have been listening to clients to better revise how we position and brand ourselves. They tell us that our micro-authoring is easy to use so we have strengthened our storytelling around being easy to use and easy to create content.

Question: Have you done any training, development, or coaching for your leaders or staff? If so, what did you do and what was the impact?

So-Young: We constantly train and develop our team using Gnowbe. We have self-directed courses, and we invest in companies like our sister company, Awaken Group, which runs our StrengthsFinder workshops every year. We invite people to as guest speakers (not often enough) and we pay for our staff to take training from other places. Learning is an extremely critical component of our work. We have had no formal coaching or leadership training, but we will soon, as we grow.

Question: What advice do you have for anyone wanting to either launch a new organization or to revitalize an existing one?

So-Young: Have patience and humility. The journey can be very tough with lots of highs and lows. You will make mistakes. Learn how to fail and pick yourself back up again. Constantly invest in yourself and your team. It may not be easy, but it can be very fulfilling and worthwhile to build something from scratch. No words can describe the joy that comes from seeing your dreams realized. That's a big part of what motivates me.

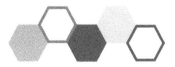

CHAPTER 7

YOUR TEAM'S PURPOSE AND DIRECTION

Once an organization's vision is clear to its founders and/or leaders, it must be converted into a written statement that provides a clear purpose and a decisive direction. This is generally called a Mission Statement, but may be called by other names. Regardless, the statement must clarify why the team/organization was formed and what it intends to accomplish in general terms. Once written, the statement will be further subdivided so others can understand how their efforts contribute to the endeavor.

The importance of this process cannot be overstated. This overarching statement guides, justifies, encompasses, and coordinates all subsequent activities for the team. When properly written, the statement provides clarity while remaining broad and uncluttered by details.

But Is It Necessary?

The purpose of many organizations seems obvious, right? Restaurants serve food, Gas Stations sell fuel, schools teach lessons, churches provide biblical insights, etc. So, isn't this just common sense? No, it is not common sense and, yes, it is necessary. Organizations are composed of people with diverse background experiences and perspectives due to differences in culture, mentoring, work history, education, training, life experiences, and more. When people assemble in a team setting, they bring all those differences with them. This influences how they think, react to stress, solve problems, bounce back from adversity, and interact with customers and coworkers alike. The result of all this diversity can be anything but predictable. Without an overarching, easy to understand, statement of purpose or mission upon which to base decisions, individuals may drift in opposite directions, thereby creating chaos instead of order. Common sense is a meaningless term unless and until common knowledge becomes common practice.

How Can I See the Big Picture When I'm Stuck Inside This Cubicle?

In today's world, it can be a challenge for some team members to understand how their efforts dovetail, compliment, and/or potentially conflict with those around them. Several generations ago, this was not the case. Artisans worked diligently from start to finish on projects such as rifles, furniture, and wagons, thereby thinking in terms of the whole. Much of this broad-based perspective has been lost in our modern-day practices of assembly lines, office cubicles, and piece-meal work. The more we separate employees, asking them to specialize, the more we must communicate with them about what is commonly called the "big picture." Failure to do so invariably forces people into compartmentalized, self-first thinking that is harmful to the overall purpose of the team.

This type of segregated environment causes people to think and act in extremes. Some believe that their efforts are insignificant, while others view their work as supremely important. Quite a contrast, and yet, each position springs from a failure to comprehend that all contributions are significant parts of the whole and are equally necessary to accomplish the mission.

No Mission = No Teamwork

Without a clear, unifying mission, it is nearly impossible to build and maintain a cohesive team. Once members of an organization feel that they and their contributions are separate from those around them, they turn inward, often with little regard for the needs of others. Self-interest and self-preservation become paramount in the minds of detached staff members. In these settings, you can be sure that when problems arise, the initial question will center on one issue—*Who is to blame?* Production blames maintenance, sales staff criticize those in public relations and marketing, the deacon board blames the elder board, some family members criticize others, and so on.

I once had the opportunity to help a pastor analyze the lack of unity among staff members of his church. After a series of face to face interviews with the staff, I learned that the combatants all genuinely wanted the church to grow and seemed to have a great deal in common. So, what was the problem? We eventually discovered that the source of their trouble was a lack of agreement on the mission. Some believed that the church should be run according to a long list of rules and regulations. To them, any violation of the rules meant expulsion from membership. Others believed that while some rules were appropriate, there should be ample room for mercy, grace, and tolerance for those yet weak in their faith. Once this significant difference was identified, the leaders were able to work together to forge a new, common understanding of the church's mission. After extensive strategic planning sessions, most of the group arrived at a new position that fell somewhere between the original two. Predictably, some were unable to accept this revised statement of mission and they resigned. While this was unfortunate, it was far better than the alternative of extended infighting, confusion, and ultimately, a split congregation.

How to Write Your Mission Statement

Your mission statement needs to have sufficient verbiage to explain the essence of why the organization exists and what it hopes to achieve or become. Before you get started with the process, there are two things you will need to battle against.

- Impatience (hurrying the process)
- Thinking one word is as good as another

If you are in a hurry to get a statement written so you can move on to the important stuff... you are missing the point. Each step in the process *IS* the important stuff. If you begin your journey without the proper direction, you may miss your destination by a mile. You must set aside sufficient time to clarify and then capture your team's purpose and direction. Often, this takes more than one sitting to accomplish.

Also, when writing your mission statement, **every word matters.** Take your time, write it out, then walk away. Come back and make sure it says what you intended. Do this until you are sure it is the correct foundational statement for your organization. All mission statements should contain directional components that clarify *what* the organization does and, essentially, why it exists. This may include information about product specialties, markets, and/or quality standards. In addition, some mission statements contain cultural components that address or define standards for both internal and external relationships and behavior.

As an example, here is the mission statement that has guided the team here at my own company.

We at Molitor International *demonstrate* and teach foundational principles of leadership, interpersonal relationships, and problem solving to unleash the dynamic potential in communities, organizations, and individuals.

Because our work focuses heavily on the development of productive interpersonal relationships, we include both the directional [What we do] and cultural [How we do it] components in our statement of mission. The directional components clarify whom we work with—communities of all sizes, organizations of all types, and individuals—and that we teach foundational principles of leadership, interpersonal relationships, and problem solving.

The cultural aspect of the statement is captured in one simple word—*demonstrate*. This word is underlined for one simple and supremely important reason: It reminds all of us that if we are not ready to actively validate our foundational values such as caring, integrity, and respect by our actions, then we are not ready to teach them to others.

One of the best mission statements I ever read comes from a large hospital system in Michigan that describes its purpose and direction with these simple words:

Extraordinary Care for Every Generation

It is amazing to watch this organization of nearly 5000 team members use this statement as the litmus test for all actions, decisions, and plans. It is not always the longest statements that are the most powerful and effective.

Whether you are writing your first mission statement for a startup or dusting off an existing one in a well-established organization, the process is the same. Bring together the leaders and/or advisers for deep discussions about the overall vision. Then, convert those discussion points into a written statement that defines your purpose and direction.

Leaders Establish the Mission

It is the founders and/or leaders of an organization that establish the guiding statements. This is *not* the job of employees, volunteers, or other team members. This may sound contrary to the concept of 'inclusion', but it is actually just the proper application of it. Team members should be invited to participate in certain decisions once the vision, mission, and values are in place. For example, staff members should be invited to take part in discussions, problem solving, and decision-making regarding issues that affect their individual or departmental roles and responsibilities. The bottom line here is the leaders of a nation, community, company, ministry, or family must establish the purpose and direction, and then create opportunities for those working under them to give input into the details of their duties.

Once a mission or purpose statement is written, it must then be effectively communicated internally and externally. All team members, customers, suppliers, volunteers, and community members need to know why the organization exists and what to expect from it. During the communication process, the statement is explained in detail so that individuals that were not part of the process can comprehend its full meaning. Those few important words are essential for all personnel to work cohesively toward their common purpose. Not only is a well-stated mission the bedrock for organizational excellence but it is also the first tangible step in the creation of a resilient team.

CHAPTER 8

ESSENTIAL STRATEGIES

Y ou have successfully identified or clarified your
team's purpose and direction, so now it is time
to launch into action, right? Buy real estate,
hire people, find volunteers, secure that web designer,
and ... whoa. Better slow down. The mission is only
the beginning or foundational step that now must be
expanded before the first brick is laid, person is hired,
or promotional poster is printed.

While this may be obvious for startups, the same is
true for existing organizations hoping to change their
trajectory. Action without direction is chaos, so let us

use our mission statement to help organize our efforts around a few essential strategies.

A Universal Concept

The concept of essential strategies applies whether you are launching a local coffee shop or revisioning an entire nation. In 1997, I was invited to lead a fascinating project for the government of Benin, Africa. The nation's President, Matthew Kerekou, had made some amazing changes in his life. Years before, he had come to power via a military coup, ruled with an iron fist, and then eventually left office. While out of office, he had a "chance" meeting with a pastor, Romain Zannou, and had a conversion to Christianity. Also, during this time, Benin rejected military rule and became a democracy.

Amazingly, in 1996, Mr. Kerekou ran for office and was elected President. With his change of heart came a change of vision for his nation. Soon, he began working with influential leaders from around the globe to improve conditions in Benin. One of those leaders was Mr. Gunnar Olson of Sweden, who reached out to me with the invitation to come to Africa to discuss "a project."

I recall sitting with Gunnar in the bright African sun, sipping coffee, with antelope and giraffe wandering by. Our first discussion went something like this:

Gunnar: "President Kerekou requests your assistance with a project for his nation."

Me: "What is the project?"

Gunnar: "He wants to identify tangible ways to show the love of God to Benin's five and a half million citizens."

Me: [stunned silence]

Gunnar: "Don't worry, we are bringing together a few hundred business leaders to help. They will be here in three days, and you will lead them in this process. I am sure it will go well."

Me: [longer stunned silence]

I confess it took some time for the request to sink in, a longer time for me to accept, and an even longer time before I had a clue how to go about it due to the magnitude of the project. However, during the three days of preparation time, one of my associates and I created the strategic plan using the same process presented in this book. We started with the mission statement that we had been given by President Kerekou: To *tangibly* show the love of God to five and a half million people in Benin.

It was clear that the overarching purpose was humanitarian, not evangelistic, but that still left a great deal to interpretation. That one word "tangibly" was key and during our planning sessions, we identified fifteen strategies, each accomplishing a part of the stated mission. These included: fresh water for remote villages, transportation, education, tourism, upgrades to utilities, and others.

Soon, we gathered with an amazing group of individuals from all around the globe to add detail to the core strategies. We put the individuals into small groups, assigned one of the strategies to each group, and asked them to identify the resources and timelines needed to implement their specific strategic goal.

I was honored to spend a week with that group of world-changers, some of whom later went to Benin to oversee the implementation of their project. When my part of the project ended, it was also an honor to meet with the French-speaking President himself and despite the language barrier, and the guards armed with sub-machine guns, I accepted his thanks and left Africa tired but happy.

Establishing Your Team's Strategies

Essential or core strategies set the mission in motion and move us from *what* we want to do or become into the next phase of *how* we will accomplish it. They force us to identify where we should focus our efforts, what is needed in terms of resources, and how we will eventually measure or progress. To show how it works, let us use the mission statement shared earlier from my own company.

Mission Statement: We at Molitor International *demonstrate* and teach foundational principles of leadership, interpersonal relationships, and problem solving to unleash the dynamic potential in communities, organizations, and individuals.

Again, the statement above explains *what* but does not explain *how* it will be accomplished. So, the following strategies were established.

1. **Strategy #1**: We will develop our own line of unique, highly interactive training materials.

2. **Strategy #2**: We will create an easy-to-use 360 survey process for assessing and coaching leaders.

3. **Strategy #3**: We will offer principle-based services that improve the overall quality of life of those we assist, including organizational, family, civic, and personal aspects of life.

4. **Strategy #4**: We will hire and train professionals who demonstrate caring for others.

5. **Strategy #5**: We will not provide short-term programs. Instead, we will seek long-term, mutually beneficial relationships with clients to see them through the entire process of transformation.

Once our strategies were in place, the next steps were much easier to identify. So, it was time to begin the hiring process, develop the materials, and hold discussions with potential clients to make sure we were aligned in our expectations. We then went about subdividing each essential strategy into component parts of the work itself as we will explore in the next chapters.

REWIRED FITNESS CO.

An interview with Adam Ludlow, Founder and CEO of Rewired Fitness Co.

Adam Ludlow launched Rewired Fitness Co. in Spokane, Washington, in 2013. He had a strong desire to own a gym and to work for himself, accepting the risks and reaping the rewards that come with entrepreneurship.

His vision was to create a unique "third place" for people through fitness. Recognizing that people spend much of their time at home and work, he wanted to create a gym that provided more than just fitness. He wanted it to be a place for people to belong to and grow healthier together. He knew it would be challenging in the already crowded fitness market in Spokane, but he dove in, did the work, and built his dream gym.

The evidence of his gym's appeal is impressive. During 2020, they matched 2019 revenue despite having to be closed for 40% of the year. Their average class size is 10.1, the average customer attends 2.75 times per week, and the average length of membership last 33 months. The gym created fourteen jobs for others in the Spokane area.

Question: What were your greatest challenges?

Adam: Probably defining our story in a saturated market. Also, in 2020, we faced the COVID shutdowns like everyone else which was very hard on us all.

Question: When times got tough, how did the concept of resilience play a part in your continued success?

Adam: To get through the tough times, I bet on myself, trusted our values, stayed fully committed to our mission, and asked experts for help.

Question: Was there a time when your team needed to be revised, transformed, or rebuilt? Explain.

Adam: Yes, in 2017 we rebranded away from CrossFit Rewired to Rewired Fitness Co. to better align our business/product with our values/story. It seemed risky at the time but ended up being a great decision.

Question: Have you done any training, development, or coaching for your leaders or staff? If so, what did you do and what was the impact?

Adam: Absolutely. Our staff has been paramount to our success. Since 2017, we have only hired from within, meaning we hired people that were part of our gym "family." That paid off for us in major ways. We have the right people in place and their live and breathe our DNA. This has been costly and timely, but it has also been 100% worthwhile.

All of my staff were asked to take various personality assessment surveys and follow-up courses. In addition, each staff member pursued and were granted various professional (coaching) certifications. At times, I brought in subject matter experts to raise our levels of expertise. All of these were critical in maintaining and retaining top professionals that are vital to this sort of organization.

Question: What advice do you have for anyone wanting to either launch a new organization or to revitalize an existing one?

Adam: Be unbelievably clear about your mission, remain 100% committed to your mission, while remaining flexible on your methods.

CHAPTER 9

HOW WORK GETS DONE

There are countless tasks that must be done properly, on time, and in the correct sequence for a team to succeed. This type of coordinated effort never happens by accident, but rather when a process is in place to link and align each member's work [tasks] with one or more essential strategy. This is true whether the task is filling a cup with coffee, tallying up the day's receipts, putting a nut on a bolt, greeting customers at the door, or putting a bandage on the skinned knee of a patient. Without these well-planned linkages, the team's core strategies are more like mini dreams with little chance of coming true.

In simplest terms, organizations of all kinds accomplish their work by following the sequence.

1. Vision/Mission. This is the launching pad for your idea that results in the creation or revision of an organization. You first envision what the organization is to do or be, and then convert that vision into a statement that is communicated to others.

2. Essential Strategies. Once the mission is clear, then you develop strategies that explain how team members are to go about achieving it. These strategies may involve product lines, locations, personnel requirements, sales, service strategies, and more. Once established, these strategic concepts are subdivided into goals and assigned to appropriate areas and/or individuals.

3. Goals. Goals are the logical, clearly defined targets that help to complete one or more essential strategy. Sometimes called objectives, these goals can be measured, monitored, corrected as needed, and celebrated when achieved.

4. Projects. Projects are activities that lead to the accomplishment of one or more goal. Each project is led by individuals who accept responsibility for their completion. Projects must be prioritized so they are done in order of importance.

5. Tasks. These are the hundreds, if not thousands, of individual activities that must be done. Each task has a correct way to be accomplished as well as a timeline and priority. Ideally, team members understand how each task helps to complete a project; how each project helps to accomplish one or more goals; how each goal is a vital part of one or more of the core strategies, that lead to the accomplishment of the team's overall mission.

Preparing the Team for Success

Leaders often make the mistake of assuming that all members understand how their work directly relates to the mission. Often, the understanding simply does not exist. When this happens, individuals can doubt the value of their contributions to the team and/or may not seek perfection in their performance. This is unfortunate and unnecessary. One of the more significant roles of leadership is to ensure that all staff members understand:

- How their efforts relate to the organization's success
- How their efforts link and align with the work of others on the team
- How each task is to be done correctly, using detailed performance standards
- *When* each task is to be done by communicating the priority and timeline associated with the task

Isn't the above simply common sense? Doesn't everyone intuitively understand how it all fits together? Of course, the answer is no: tasks need to be explained in detail, or errors will occur jeopardizing projects, goals, strategies, and the mission itself. This does *not* mean that leaders must spend every waking hour hovering over team members, frantically communicating all the above information. Since many tasks are repetitive and/or similar, this sort of information is initially given during the team member's onboarding, again during job training, and may be repeated throughout the year, especially if performance problems arise.

The legendary football coach, Vince Lombardi, was said to have begun each year's practice by holding up a ball and announcing to his world-champion players... "Team, this is a football." From there, he and his assistant coaches went on to explain to each player the minute details of their "tasks" that would lead to another championship months later.

The Finishing Touch: Why?

Insightful leaders not only explain to team members what and how a task is to be done, but also *why* the task is to be done. Remember that each of us is seeking purpose in life and part of that purpose is often found in our work. So, if a staff person or volunteer sees his or her work as mundane, isolated from the rest of the "important" things being done, that becomes demotivating. In sharp contrast, when someone understands that his or her efforts are vital parts of the whole, then the opposite happens, resulting in motivation and greater levels of engagement.

Once you have provided proper instructions about goals, projects, and individual tasks, it is wise to listen to staff ideas about *how* to get these things accomplished. After an initial learning period, team members obtain new perspectives about their work that may go well beyond that of their leaders. Leaders that respectfully communicate and listen to others, especially during times of rapid and unpredictable change, often gain new insights that help in the pursuit of the mission. This approach releases the power of agreement in a profound way. That is how work gets done.

CHAPTER 10

DEFINING SUCCESS, MEASURING RESULTS

O nce your mission is clear, strategies are in place, goals are set, projects launched, and tasks are assigned, then the next logical step is to determine how to measure the team's performance and progress. This step accomplishes multiple important things, such as:

- Letting the team know when they are on track

- Letting the team know when they are getting off track

- Building resiliency by showing team capabilities over time

- Creating a record of performance upon which to base future projects, investments, adjustments, expansion and more

There are many options for this performance tracking process, but regardless of which measures you use, recording your progress and performance is essential for long-term success. The criteria you select will be called your **measures of success**.

In essence, your measures of success are the targets, and your goals, projects, and tasks are the arrows. How close actual performance comes to the bullseye provides you with important data about your overall strategy and provides vital information, such as: How profitable is your organization? How engaged are your employees? How consistent is your quality? How satisfied are your customers? These are all questions that can be answered using your measures of success.

While each organization is unique, there are some common measures of success that may include the following.

Customer Service and Satisfaction

This measure of success may be calculated in several ways. Repeat customers, customer complaints, new business, or attendance at events, to name a few. Regardless of the organization, you likely have customers of one type or another, and customers generally have choices. If you are the only game in town, then people must play at your location even if they are not treated well. However, when customers have options, they will always go where their needs are met *and* where they are treated with respect.

Quality

Quality, like customer service, is a vital component of every team's success. Whether you provide a product, service, or information, each can be measured for overall quality. For example, school districts interested in quality improvement can measure the test scores of their graduating seniors. Hospitals can measure cases of sepsis or falls. Communities can develop a quality-of-life index for crime, infant survival rate, poverty, new business start-ups, and so on.

Once the quality has been defined and baseline measurements are established, then plans may be devised to improve the performance of each area. Quality problems may be caught at the end of a process, but it is much better to build quality during the process itself and this approach requires input from those closest to the work. The bottom line on the topic of quality is simple: Any organization that fails to measure, evaluate, and improve its product and/or service quality puts itself at risk.

Productivity

Productivity and quality have a unique relationship. While quality improvement seeks to make something better, productivity improvement seeks to make something faster, in larger quantities, cheaper, and/or with fewer resources.

Regardless of the approach, organizations that achieve the greatest gains in productivity [and in quality] are those that obtain improvement input from staff at all levels. In the corporate world, this input is often obtained during informal meetings or during employee surveys. At other times, the input is given in formal structures such as empowerment programs, employee engagement teams, natural work groups, and process improvement RIE teams.

Waste, Rejects, and "Mulligans"

The worldwide concern for protecting and restoring our environment has focused attention on the broad topic of waste reduction, whether removing plastic from our oceans or cleaning up the water delivery system in municipalities. Waste and/or rejects cost money, sometimes a great deal of money.

In 2014, a decision was made to switch the water supply for the city of Flint, Michigan, from Lake Huron to the Flint River, in hopes of saving some $5 million per year. However, the move necessitated some additional treatment of the water to prevent pipes from corroding. This would have added minimal additional cost per day and amazingly, the additional treatment was not approved. As a result, lead and other harmful chemicals were released into citizens' homes, which made many residents sick. After multiple lawsuits, the city, state, and federal governments spent millions of dollars replacing pipes throughout the city, a settlement was reached and affected citizens received over $600,000,000 ... and the city's water source was moved back to Lake Huron.

I was once invited to evaluate a company that made candles in the Midwestern US. During the initial plant tour, I stopped to watch a woman that served as the final inspector for one line of candles. On either side of her were boxes into which she placed the candles after a quick inspection. After several minutes, I observed that the box on her left filled rapidly while the box on her right remained nearly empty. The ratio seems to be about 20:1. Impressed, I complimented her on the overflowing box of "good" candles. Without taking her eyes off her work, she laughed and said, "Sorry mister, but those are the rejects!" Then, she matter-of-factly explained that twice each hour another employee came by, picked up the box of rejects, and then unceremoniously dumped them all back into a vat to be melted down for another try ... *mulligans*, she called them. When I asked how long that practice had been tolerated, she smiled again and said, "As long as I have been here."

It is not clear to me whether the candle company is the exception or the rule, but one thing is sure; organizations interested in making positive change in this area must challenge their enemies of status quo and precedent. Waste is an indicator that something is wrong and needs to be fixed.

Growth

Organizational growth is a two-edged sword. Growth is generally seen as a good thing, so wise leaders watch for expansion opportunities such as enlarging existing facilities, adding new product lines, expanding services, and/or diversifying. However, growth must be well planned and balanced to prevent destabilizing existing operations and/or causing the organization to compromise quality, profitability, or customer service.

One of our corporate clients barely survived a bout of unmanaged growth several years ago. They launched a new product that really took off in the marketplace. Soon, their workforce ballooned from two hundred to over six hundred employees as the new product resulted in unprecedented—and unplanned for—demand. The downside of the growth was the organization had nowhere to put all the new people. Makeshift desks and workstations sprang up like mushrooms after a spring rain. The communication system was inadequate, so customer calls were lost. Frustrations expanded faster than the new product sales.

Predictably, many of the new customers were exasperated by the poor service and terrible communication, and the new product line faltered. The leaders of that company focused so intently on whether it *could* grow that it failed to consider whether it *should* grow. Growth and expansion are measures of success, but only if managed properly.

Profitability

A wonderful old song tells us that *Love makes the world go around.* While that may be true, it takes money to do most everything else. Virtually every organization on earth needs some sort of revenue stream to function. Once your team is up and running, it has two methods to better itself financially. It can lower its costs, or it can increase incoming revenues. Profit is not a dirty word, and no for-profit organization should ever apologize for making money from its operations. Profitability is a legitimate measure of team success.

Employee Engagement and Staff Retention

People that are content in their jobs tend to stay. People that are not content tend to leave. In the past, people often started working for one company and a quarter of a century later retired, receiving a gold watch and an assurance of monthly pension checks for life. Today, not so much. Faithful employees *might* be handed watches on their way out, but the money stops as soon as the door closes behind them.

According to the Bureau of Labor Statistics, in the year 2022, the median number of years that both blue and white-collar workers remain with their employers is approximately four years. Is this a big deal, especially since there are others out there that might take the departing person's place? It is an extremely big deal ... Statistics also show that the cost of replacing an employee ranges from 50% to 150% of that person's annual compensation. This means that a revolving door in your organization costs you thousands if not hundreds of thousands of dollars. It is infinitely better to hire great people, bring them into a positive culture, treat them fairly, and retain them.

Your Sense of Peace, Joy, and Contentment

I saved this one for last because it requires the most thought. Whether you are the team's founder or you joined an existing organization, work is the place where you likely spend most of your waking hours. It is the place where your gifts and talents are utilized, your legacy is built, your resiliency is honed, and your livelihood is secured.

In the grand scheme of things, the organization is part of your identity and the degree to which you are content in the context of it has a lot to do with your overall quality of life. An important measure of success is how *you* feel about *your* role, *your* accomplishments, and how being part of the team fits into *your* overall balance in life. This is the one measure of success that will not make it onto a monthly report, but will be seen and felt by you and those closest to you for a lifetime. How successful are you?

We Are Now Ready to Get to Work, Right?

At this point, you have organized the critical elements for your team's success. Your mission is established, your strategies are in place, your goals and projects are set, and tasks are supported with clear standards, priorities, and timelines. This means that everyone knows what to do, how to do it, and even why it is to be done. Success is just around the corner, right? Sorry...not exactly. The reason for the concern is summed up in two words...*human nature.*

Teams are made up of people and, as we covered in earlier chapters, human beings have amazing capacities for creativity, cooperation, problem-solving and so much more. However, human beings are also capable of just the opposite. Some hate change, others refuse to work well with teammates, some cause more problems than they solve. Individuals are also capable of misunderstanding each other, hurting each other, becoming self-centered, causing conflict and other disruptive behaviors. So, the team may have the most compelling mission, the greatest strategies, clear-cut goals and projects, and incredibly detailed tasks, but if the team's relationships break down, none of that matters. This is where the subjects of culture, core values, and commitment come in. It is the combination of meticulously organized work *and* a well-designed culture that leads to resilience and success for teams of all types.

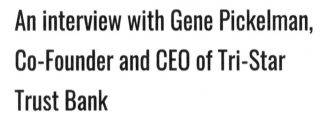

SUCCESS STORY:
TRI-STAR TRUST BANK

An interview with Gene Pickelman, Co-Founder and CEO of Tri-Star Trust Bank

When CEO Gene Pickelman and his partner founded Tri-Star Trust Bank in 2000, it had very humble beginnings. A few phones, desks, and file cabinets in a small, rented office. The vision was for a client-centered firm that would take a genuine, personal interest in its clients, employees, and the community.

After more than twenty years and a great deal of hard work, the organization has grown beyond the founders' dreams and become a powerhouse in this extraordinarily complex industry. Through strong relationships and an intentional purpose, Tri-Star Trust Bank has grown to a staff of more than 40 professionals, managing over $1.6 billion in client assets, contributing to more than 160 local nonprofits, and expanding to four locations in Michigan.

They now offer services in financial planning, investment management, trust administration, corporate retirement planning, and philanthropic solutions for clients. Their overarching statement of purpose is stated this way "building caring, genuine relationships that strengthen families and transform our communities."

Question: What were your greatest challenges?

Gene: My greatest challenge was trying to be patient when it came to building new clients. Many of us had over 20 years of experience in the field, but we were a new institution. People wanted to be with an established institution. I truly felt we had a high quality, competitively priced service, but we often came in second.

Question: When times got tough, how did the concept of resilience play a part in your continued success?

Gene: Keeping the focus on serving our clients, doing the right things, and let the results come. Our board support and encouragement were key. They never lost confidence in us, as leaders of the organization.

Question: Was there a time when your team needed to be revised, transformed, or rebuilt? Explain.

Gene: Yes, we needed to get better at what we did, including better systems, communications, servicing . . . process improvement continuously. We were never afraid of asking, can we do this better? We also needed to take a good look at how we were treating our staff . . . we needed to be more attentive to their feelings, attitudes, and opportunities for personal growth.

Question: Have you done any training, development, or coaching for your leaders or staff? If so, what did you do and what was the impact?

Gene: Yes . . . many of our staff went through the Molitor 1000 Leaders program and this shaped our business model of establishing great relationships both internally and externally. We had several training programs on leadership training and coaching. We hired Brian D. Molitor and others to train our staff members. This was invaluable. We needed to be consistent with the training. This was a challenge because of the time and the expense, but if you do not train your people, you will never reach your full potential. This resulted in high employee satisfaction and engagement, as well as increased creativity and innovation.

Question: What advice do you have for anyone wanting to either launch a new organization or to revitalize an existing one?

Gene: Find your higher purpose. When making decisions, consider all stakeholders. Never trade off. Build a conscious culture, one that inspires people and gives them an opportunity to grow, learn and develop. Build leaders. You must trust and depend on your leadership team.

CHAPTER 11

CORE VALUES

In previous chapters, we covered concepts of mission, goals, projects, and tasks that provide operational *direction* for a team's work. This is a good beginning; however, organizations must also design and define their *culture*, which is the human side of the equation.

Core values are the foundational building blocks of a team's culture. They could also be called the standards or principles that define the "rights and wrongs" or "dos and don'ts" that members of the team are expected to adhere to. Within each organization, there must be clarity around what is acceptable and unacceptable behavior or else a sort of "everyone for themselves" paradigm kicks in, leading to self-centered, near anarchistic, unproductive behavior. Leaders who fail to clarify their expectations related to core values find themselves serving as referees between feuding staff members or struggling to explain a team member's rude behavior to a valued client who is headed out the door.

This concept of core values and their accompanying consequences, positive or negative, are not new to us as each day, we are subject to norms, rules, statutes, and laws from multiple sources. During early years, young people learn the benefits . . . or consequences related to household chores, homework assignments, and how siblings are treated. Later in life come the rewards or consequences of adherence to societal and organizational rules. Get caught drunk driving and you pay a price. Show up late for work continually and you may lose your job. Show respect for those around you and develop friendships, remain diligent and professional and you stand a good chance for promotion. So, whether in the home, school, work, or in society at large, we learn the rules and either abide by them and prosper or risk the probability of negative consequences.

The Case for Core Values

After nearly four decades in the field of human resource development, I have observed that people either raise or lower their behaviors to established standards. Within organizations where there are no set core values, individuals tend to disintegrate into factions, creating their own subcultures with differing standards of behavior toward leaders, coworkers, customers, and the work itself. The negative impact of these diverse "standards" [actually lack of standards] is profound. Adversarial labor-management relations, sexual harassment, workplace dishonesty, and low customer satisfaction often find their roots in the soil of unclear culture and/or conflicting core values.

Core values reveal the heart and character of an organization as quickly as they reveal the heart and character of a person. Consider this...Adolph Hitler's stated *mission* for his country sounded good. It included national pride, high levels of employment, and prosperity for all. At first glance, it would be difficult for anyone to find fault with what he proposed. However, when Hitler's *core values* of hatred, prejudice, lust for power, and ultimately genocide, are seen along with his mission, the picture becomes clear of how he sought to accomplish his twisted dream. Core values and mission are inseparable and must be aligned. The mission is the desired end, and the core values are the cultural means to that end.

It is important to note that core values are different from employee handbooks and employment contracts. Plato, the ancient philosopher, said, "Good people do not need laws to tell them to act responsibly, while bad people will find a way around the laws ... " While he was speaking about society in general, his comment has application for teams as well. Here is why. Many organizations have employee handbooks that *try* to list all the policies to be followed. Here is the problem. Even though these handbooks are detailed and cumbersome, they can never anticipate every situation to be faced. As our friend Plato indicated, there are always a few individuals that look for ways to "game" the system for personal gain.

The problems and challenges that face organizations today require much more than a simple interpretation of the rules by some corporate referee. To remain competitive, we must solve problems in the framework of an organization's mission, strategies, *and* its core values that allows for flexibility rather than just a hard and fast set of rules.

Every so often, I hear an objection to the creation of core values by someone who declares that "you can't dictate morality." While I agree that organizations cannot dictate morality or ethics, they *can* create and enforce standards of behavior through their clearly stated core values. In other words, ethics and morality are internal issues that come from within each person's heart—only God can change that. However, professional, ethical, and moral behavior can be *influenced* within an organization when there are clear definitions of what is acceptable and unacceptable, and when people receive appropriate rewards or consequences for their actions.

How to Create Your Team's Core Values

Your core values may be recorded as a list of individual words, or short phrases such as *Honesty, Integrity,* and *Caring for others.* Alternatively, they may be arranged in an all-encompassing sentence or short paragraph. For example, at Molitor International, we use the following statement to highlight our company's core values [The terms that identify our core values are highlighted in bold for emphasis]:

We strive to be known by our customers, suppliers, coworkers, and others as people of **integrity, honesty, caring, respect, faith**, and **professionalism**.

The development of core values is a serious a matter and the responsibility lies with the leadership of the organization. This is not a task that can be delegated to others, nor is it a participative process whereby every employee, parishioner, or family member gets a vote. Much like the mission and essential strategies of the organization, the core values are developed by the leaders and then communicated to the rest of the organization. However, there is a vitally important role for others to play as will be explained below.

When assisting clients with this process, I have each member of the leadership group independently write out his or her words, terms, and concepts that describe their desired core values on paper or laptops. Then, one by one, each explains his or her ideas until all have been covered. This approach prevents "group thinking" where one individual mentions a word or concept and all others immediately support it without first independently identifying what they believe should be on the final list.

From five to seven core values are sufficient to capture what leadership intends and that number is easy for team members to remember and apply. At times, organizations get carried away and approach this process much like the creation of an employee handbook, trying to cover every possible situation. When this happens, they may end up with ten to fifteen "core" values and that simply does not work. That many concepts are difficult to remember and apply, which is the reason for creating the list of core values in the first place.

Once all words and terms have been discussed, the group then identifies the most important ones for their team to focus on. This may require some wordsmithing, a bit of compromise, and even referring to a dictionary to discern the full meaning of a concept. Eventually, a final list of terms is settled on and the team's core values are now in place. This is cause for celebration, but the process is not quite finished.

Creating Clarity about Core Values

Because core values are often represented by a single word or short phrase, additional detail is needed to ensure understanding throughout the team. This is because words, even common ones, mean different things to different people. For example, if a person says: I *love* my spouse, I *love* apple fritters, and I *love* to travel, would you know what was meant by the word *love*?

Here is another example. The term *honesty* is a core value that often makes it onto a team's list. To most people, the word means: to tell the truth, to deal fairly with others, to respect other's property, and so on. However, there are people that think *brutal* honesty is a virtue and have no problem humiliating others by ripping apart their ideas, their suggestions, or their performance, all in the name of *honesty*. So, given these different interpretations, is honestly a good or a bad quality in a team environment? Here is a hint . . . it is a good quality for any team *provided* there is shared understanding of what it means in that context.

The way to prevent misunderstandings of core values is by clearly defining them through the use of *accountable actions*.

How Accountable Actions Work

If leaders select *honesty* as one of their core values, then they must define the term and communicate it to all members of the team. This is accomplished by creating a series of statements that convert the concept into actions. Here are a few examples of how it is done using three additional core values.

Core Value #1: Working Together. I will build and maintain positive, supportive relationships with those around me.

Core Value #2: Respect. I will value and show appreciation for the personal dignity and diversity of others, treating them with kindness and compassion.

Core Value #3: Enthusiasm. I will show passion and positivity in my work and all my interactions with others.

This process is followed for each core value until all have been described by easy-to-understand phrases.

Unlike the creation of the mission statement, team members can help convert core values into actions.

This is as simple as asking team members to describe things that can be done or avoided so that attitudes, behaviors, and communications are aligned with the values.

One of my favorite clients in West Virginia used a unique approach by combining core values and accountable actions into a single list. Executive leadership first identified the primary core values. Then, they invited staff to participate in word-smithing activities to add more details and create the list of accountable actions. Here is what they produced:

We believe that every employee should:

1. Conduct ourselves in a positive manner.

2. Foster cooperation rather than confrontation.

3. Communicate in a positive and helpful manner— avoid propagating rumors and other forms of negative communication.

4. Promote doing the right thing instead of focusing on one's need to be right.

5. Recognize and appreciate others.

The creators of this list are some of the toughest, most independent people I have ever met, yet they overcame generations of combative, win/lose thinking to forge a new way of organizational life. Both management and employees recognized that clear core values and accountable actions were the best way to focus energies on satisfying customers rather than fighting against each other. In the years following their cultural change, the value of their company skyrocketed.

Embedding Core Values into the Fabric of the Team

The next step in the process is to regularly communicate the new core values and accountable actions to every member of the team so the culture can begin to build. This is not done via an email blast, nor is it sufficient to hold a single meeting to discuss the values and then forget about them. Instead, the core values must now become a topic of regular conversation, presentation, and review throughout the organization. Staff meetings are great places for the values to be regularly presented and discussed so there is no drift in expectations.

Eventually, the core values and accountable actions will be institutionalized as they are used during the hiring process, onboarding new staff, evaluating performance, disciplinary action, and for identifying those that qualify for promotion.

What is of ultimate importance with core values and accountable actions is that all members of the organization understand what is acceptable in terms of their attitudes, behaviors, communications, and decisions. These are the issues that define the culture, and it is culture that either leads to or leads away from success. It is also that consistent culture that provides the stability, confidence and hope during even the roughest stretches on the journey. The result is resilience.

Now, there is one final foundational concept that must be developed to solidify your culture . . . leadership expectations.

CHAPTER 12

LEADERSHIP EXPECTATIONS

A t this point in the process, you have clarity around your organization's purpose, direction, and culture. So, what is next? As the team begins to function, someone or some group must take responsibility for overall performance and that is a primary function of those in leadership. In a perfect world, each member of the team would self-manage, stay focused on priority tasks, work well with others, and keep themselves motivated . . . but ours is not a perfect world. It is the leadership group that has the sacred duty of focusing on the mission, protecting the culture, demonstrating

the core values, managing the work, and supporting all
other members of the team.

Leadership: The Foundation of Success

Historically, organizational charts are presented in the
form of a pyramid, with the most senior leaders at the
top and staff with the least amount of authority at the
base. This may look good on paper, but it is upside down
from how teams actually function. In fact, leaders are
the *base* upon which the rest of the organization is built.
A weak leadership base cannot support staff, customers,
or communities for any length of time. In contrast, a
strong leadership base provides the stability for a team's
growth and expansion. Before going any farther, it's
important to define what is meant by 'strong' leadership.
In this case, it does not mean dictatorial, loud, force-
ful, or any other sort of external measure of strength.
Instead, strong means things like mature, professional,
fair, consistent, ethical, caring, and honest.

Of all these qualities, consistency may be the toughest for leadership teams to demonstrate. Regardless

of the title used by your leaders, whether supervisor, manager, executive, pastor, director, coach, team leader, or any other, the people in those roles share one thing in common . . . they are still people. As we have explored, people join the team with diverse backgrounds, education, experiences, biases, role models, and more. This means it is highly likely that there are inconsistencies in the way individual leaders approach motivation, accountability, discipline, communication, respect, and scores of other important aspects of leadership. Does this matter to the team? It has been said that "variety is the spice of life'" and in many instances, I am sure that is true. However, when it comes to leadership principles and behaviors, variety or variance among leaders can be very disruptive and potentially destructive.

No human being wants to come to work for a volatile or inconsistent leader who may act like a saint one day and the next as a reincarnated Attila the Hun. In addition, any inconsistencies between how policies are administered by leaders of different areas create the perception of favoritism, an extremely divisive practice.

I recently counseled a young manager who was enticed to leave his job at one large healthcare system to join another. The pitch given by his new boss was compelling, more money, better benefits, opportunities for promotion, work from home flexibility, and more. During the 'wine and dine' phase of the courtship, the young manager was taken to lunch, his past record of success was highly praised, and he was told that his skill at innovative process improvement was desperately needed at the new place of employment. So far, so good. The manager was convinced that heaven was shining upon him, so he gave a month's notice and soon joined the new company. After a few weeks on the job, he approached his new supervisor with several innovations that would improve performance and employee engagement. To his surprise, his new boss made it very clear that rather than any new ideas, he would simply need to put in 12-hour days, plus weekends to get things done the old way. The dream quickly turned into a nightmare for the young manager who realized that the sweet words he'd heard during the courtship were nothing more than manipulation on the part of his new supervisor. He lasted four months before moving on. Personalities can be deceptive, practiced principles cannot.

Clearly, each of us develops our own personality which makes the world a more interesting place. Leaders may be upbeat and happy; leaders may be quiet and more reserved; leaders may have extremely different personalities. However, the accepted diversity ends there. Leaders must interact with team members using agreed upon principles, or they risk causing dissention, dissatisfaction, and even defections within the team. Fortunately, there is a way to prevent that from happening. Clearly defined *leadership expectations* help ensure that leader actions are linked, aligned and consistent.

Leadership Expectations

Leadership expectations are written principles that are in addition to the organization's statements of mission and core values, however, they are never in conflict with them. Remember, these expectations are not personality-based, meaning they do not seek to make all leaders charismatic, funny, upbeat or any other trait. Instead, the leadership expectations address what I call the A, B, C's. These are the Attitude, Behaviors, and Communications from the leaders.

Recently, I helped a client going through the revisioning process to create a set of leadership expectations. We brought together senior and middle level leaders for extended times of brainstorming, processing, wordsmithing, and review. Eventually, the group settled on a short list of leadership expectations. Here are several that they chose and the explanations that remove any ambiguity for current and future leaders that join the team.

- **Innovation.** The ability to think outside current practices to identify innovative solutions that motivate others and accomplish core strategies.

- **Interpersonal skills.** The ability to have gracefully honest communication with others; demonstrate effective listening, teamwork, relationship building, and celebration.

- **Results.** The ability to set appropriate targets, properly delegate tasks, and use resources wisely to achieve goals in a timely manner.

Making Leadership Expectations Real

Whether the leadership expectations are created for a startup organization or are used in the transformation of an existing one, the process for making them integral parts of the culture is the same. Once the founders and/ or top-level leaders create the expectations, then they do the following:

1. Bring together all leaders and communicate the expectations, making sure there is time for questions to clarify anything that is unclear.

2. Provide training in the expectations to make sure that all leaders possess the skill and will to implement them daily.

3. Provide coaching and mentoring to any leaders that struggle with demonstrating the expectations.

4. Begin to use the leadership expectations as standards when evaluating, rewarding, promoting, and dismissing those in positions of authority.

5. Use the leadership expectations to provide clear, consistent guidelines for hiring, training, and mentoring new leaders so that they can continue to build the desired culture by their actions.

MAGMA GEMS CUSTOM FINE JEWELRY

An interview with Andrew Forester, founder and CEO of Magma Gems Custom Fine Jewelry

Magma Gems Custom Fine Jewelry, located in Saginaw, Michigan, was established in 1979 and rode the corporate roller coaster of highs and lows for many years. The organization was re-envisioned in 2017 when Andrew Forester purchased the business and began the process of cultural transformation.

The decision to purchase went against conventional wisdom as more than 1200 jewelry stores go out of business each year. Andrew and his team of professionals immediately began to change the culture using the foundations of treating customers with great respect, performing only high-quality work, and charging fair prices for their custom-made jewelry.

As a result of the revisioning, the business grew by 40% in a very short time. Also, as a result of increased focus on their customers' experience, Magma's online reviews went from an average of 3.0 with multiple negative comments in a row to an average rating of 4.7 and fifty 5-star ratings.

Question: What were your greatest challenges?

Andrew: Mine were mostly internal struggles. I had to battle the fear of past failures, and the sense that I might have just left my security and boarded a sinking ship. The staff I inherited seemed old and tired. Also, I was known in our community by my previous roles in other businesses, so I was not sure if I would be taken seriously in this new identity as a craftsman.

Question: When times got tough, how did the concept of resilience play a part in your continued success?

Andrew: When each tough time came . . . and there were many of them, I'd say out loud "I trust you Lord." Also, each time I felt hopeless I would say "something good is about to happen." In those stressful times, I would do my best and at the end of the day, He would give me peace to sleep. The next day, I would get up and much of the time, something good *did* happen.

Question: What are you most proud of?

Andrew: Probably the best part was building trust in an existing team of older pessimists and seeing them get excited for their futures in the business. On a broader scale, I am proud of our efforts to revamp an entire business philosophy, business structure, and culture. Watching the business increase by 40% was the icing on the cake. Also, after many arguments with staff about how important it is to treat customers with kindness and respect, it was great to watch them change and to see the resulting increase in customer satisfaction.

Question: Was there a time when your team needed to be revised, transformed, or rebuilt? Explain.

Andrew: This had to happen the minute I bought the business. With over 1200 jewelry stores a year going out of business each year, I figured we had a short time to revise the entire model. I knew we could make beautiful jewelry, but without a transformation of how the business operated, we would have been number 1201. Once the new culture was in place, I breathed easier.

Question: Have you done any training, development, or coaching for your leaders or staff? If so, what did you do and what was the impact?

Andrew: Retraining was key to our success. Remember, we had incredibly talented jewelers on staff, but our customer service was poor. That was the most important thing that needed to change. As the new owner, I realized that action speaks volumes over words, and I had to *BE* the culture I expected to see from others. After a full year, staff came around. In year two, there were still some conflicts, yet with written core values and operating principles, our staff accepted, applied, and began to see the benefits of the changes. In year three, I was able to hire new people with the new protocol already in place and they helped support the new culture.

Question: What advice do you have for anyone wanting to either launch a new organization or to revitalize an existing one?

Andrew: Volunteer first in the industry, business, or ministry you want to pursue before you dive in. Once you take the plunge, do not expect immediate positive change. No matter how good it sounds or how much it makes sense. Put your requirements, expectations, values, and principles in writing to set your new standards. Then, you must faithfully *BE* the revitalization. No cheating, staff and customers are watching your EVERY move to see if you can and will uphold your own expectations. When dealing with existing staff that was used to a different culture, make sure you sincerely credit ALL positive change from them. Slowly but surely, the culture will adjust.

Finally, if you buy an existing business that is not making tons of money...then do NOT quit your day job. Expect to work 60–80 hours a week as you make the transition. Financially, do not expect to be paid more than your employees until the new changes prove effective and the additional business provides more income thus justifying a personal raise. Until then, cut back your personal expenses, not the expenses of the business.

CHAPTER 13

DEVELOPING YOUR LEADERS

L eaders are the foundation upon which an organization is built. Of course, this does not mean that other members of the organization have lessor value or that other factors are not important. I describe leadership as the delightful burden. Those in positions of authority must protect the vision, demonstrate the core values, live the leadership expectations, while carrying the responsibility for a significant portion of the organization's success. Delightful. Burden.

Just as effective leaders are foundations for a team's success, ineffective leaders put organizations at great risk.

Years ago, I saw this truth played out while working with a warehouse client in Ohio. It seems that one day, the employees walked in and saw the following sign on their bulletin board:

EFFECTIVE IMMEDIATELY

Employees will no longer work together when loading trucks.

At first, the employees thought that it might be a prank, but it was not. Two neophyte managers had placed it there to address what they saw as serious problems within the work environment. The rationale for their new policy? The previous day, the young supervisors observed two employees laughing as they loaded unwieldy building materials onto a flatbed trailer. Laughing at work... Oh, the horror! The organization's measures of success which included productivity, delivery to customers, safety, and employee engagement had been historically high before the new policy was instituted.

Naturally, the workers were furious about this decision and responded with what I call "malicious compliance." In other words, they followed the new guidelines even though they knew it would be bad for the company.

As weeks passed, the previously profitable company began to falter. The work pace slowed dramatically, causing productivity to fall. Simultaneously, the cost of damaged goods skyrocketed since much of the material required two men to stabilize it during the loading process. Lost-time injuries began to mount as employees strained backs and tempers trying to muscle unwieldy items onto trucks.

When this madness finally came to the attention of the owner, the embarrassed young supervisors were forced to relent, but much was lost in the interim. Productivity, morale, customer satisfaction, safety, management credibility, and workplace unity were compromised during the junior 'leaders' ' short-term reign of organizational terror.

What Went Wrong?

Every problem has a cause and, in the case above, the cause was three-fold.

1. The young supervisors were untrained and unprepared to be left on their own to manage the organization's most valuable resources, its people.

2. The young supervisors lacked proper oversight by a more senior leader who should have provided mentoring *before* the mess happened.

3. The organization did not use their statements of mission, values and/or leadership expectations to provide direction for its leaders. This left each leader to set his or her own standards.

Leadership: The Heart of the Matter

Leadership is more art than a science, and it is infinitely more than simple techniques or buzzwords to get others to perform. Instead, it is a complex combination of productive attitudes, behaviors, values, and principles which must be consistently demonstrated to help others in the pursuit of a mission.

While leadership is one of the most challenging and frustrating undertakings on earth, it is also one of the most rewarding. I am convinced that anyone can learn to be an effective leader if he or she chooses to do so. Those that answer the call to lead will discover that the gap between frustration and reward is generally quite small. However, by the application of a few foundational concepts, most leaders can stay closer to the reward side of the equation.

With all that is written about the subject, it may be difficult for people to decide what their top leadership priorities should be. Goal setting? Communication? Budgeting? Problem solving? How about planning and organizing? These are all good and certainly part of a leader's toolbox, however, none of them comes close to being the most important. After teaching this subject for nearly four decades, I know that the most crucial area for a leader to focus on is the attitude of his or her heart toward those that work 'for' them. Specifically, do they see their position of leadership as an opportunity to serve or to be served? Do they genuinely care about the people they oversee or is the focus more on productivity and profits? That is the heart of the matter, an element missing in far too many discussions about leadership.

In every leadership seminar I facilitate, I ask the attendees one simple question about themselves as leaders—*do you genuinely care about your employees, volunteers, or congregation?* This forces them to consider whether the people they lead are viewed as human beings, filled with dynamic power to change the world around them, or as something less than that, perhaps no more than names or numbers on paper. The room usually gets quiet as the leaders ponder their responses. Fortunately, many realize that they do care about others within their organizations. A smaller number decide that they had never thought about it before. Amazingly, mercifully, an even smaller number admits that they really *do not* care all that much about others, and see people more as means to a better bottom-line or to further their own ambitions.

Leadership Development

Organizational leaders are no different from any other employee, volunteer, or member in that they walked through the door on the first day armed only with their past experiences, education, and insights. This means that they likely have some deficiencies that can be, must be, addressed. This is especially true in teams that promote from within. In these settings, the best technical performer is often promoted to a supervisory position where he or she may flounder unless properly trained. The options for developing a leader's capabilities include the following:

- A proper orientation process that includes discussion of the organization's mission, values, leadership expectations and more.
- Job shadowing with a senior leader.
- Regular one-on-one mentoring sessions with his or her supervisor to receive feedback on early performance.
- Customized training courses in leadership as defined by the organization's leadership expectations.
- Fast Track, one-day refreshers on the organization's core strategies, measures of success, and cultural statements.
- 360 surveys to uncover blind spots in the leader's character, interpersonal skills, and/or performance.
- Personal coaching with a professional coach.

Any of the above will help a leader to assimilate into the organization and to live by the established leadership expectations. Implementing all the above is even better.

What about leaders that have been in their positions for a longer period? Should they take part in leadership development activities? Absolutely! I've been a golfer for more than 40 years, so given that much experience, I certainly don't need any instruction . . . or do I? I still can't hit the ball straight down a fairway. Doing something for a long period of time means nothing if you have been doing it incorrectly. None of us have it completely sorted out and we all fall short at times, even in some of the basics of leadership. Some would say that "you can't teach an old dog new tricks." My response is "who would appreciate a new trick more than an old dog?" All organizational leaders should attend training sessions, receive 360 feedback, and have the opportunity take counsel from professional coaches to keep them functioning at the highest levels.

First A, Then B, Then C

It is extremely important to follow the steps laid out in this book in order. Before you design any training or development for leaders, you must first have a basis for that training. This means having a clear mission, core values, and especially clear *leadership expectations*. Failure to do so would be likened to asking a sharpshooter to hit a bull's-eye without first providing a target. He may use up a lot of ammunition and make a lot of noise but will never succeed.

Each year, countless organizations launch "leadership training" programs without first establishing their own leadership expectations. This always results in a general program of concepts taught without any long-term context. This approach is a waste of time and money. However, once the mission, values and leadership expectations are established, then developmental initiatives can easily be created. When we develop our team's leaders, the foundation is laid, and it is time to build the team.

CHAPTER 14

UNIFYING THE TEAM

My working definition of a team is: *Two or more people who are prepared, equipped, and committed to work together to achieve a common purpose.* This definition makes known that a team may be a family, school system, corporation, or even a nation that seeks to maximize its influence and effectiveness. In addition, a team may be an entire organization, or a just part of the organization. For example, the members of a local church, including the leaders, may be considered a team. However, subgroups of the same church can also be considered teams. There may be teams of ushers, teachers, preschool workers, maintenance personnel, deacons, and elders who help achieve the overall mission as they complete their own group's goals.

Often, there is confusion about the goal of a team-building effort. The concept of *teamwork* deals with productive attitudes, enhanced interpersonal relationships, and shared commitment to a goal. Conversely, the concept of *work teams* relates more to new structures and reporting relationships. Obviously, there is a huge difference between the two.

Companies throughout the world arrange their employees in a wide variety of configurations, including a modified pyramid structure, multidisciplinary task force, self-directed workgroups, product teams, and cross-functional work teams. People in these new structures may fight like cats and dogs, and yet still be called a "team." All too often, these new structures yield few positive results. The real value comes when organizational leaders find ways to develop *teamwork* among the members of their organizations. Regardless of the structure or configuration of the employees, once people learn and apply the principles of effective teamwork, then all heaven breaks loose. Then, and only then, are they able to achieve peak performance as they communicate, listen, respect, trust, resolve conflicts, and solve problems together.

Relational Breakdowns

Relationships within organizations are much like Forrest Gump's box of chocolates . . . you never know what you are going to get. Some team members work well with everyone, others cannot seem to get along with anyone. But why? Shouldn't the common mission, shared strategies, and common core values make it easy to cooperate?

Team relationships are impacted by a myriad of issues including stresses from deadlines, budgets, conflicts over resources, professional and positional jealousy, prejudice of all sorts, and basic personality conflicts. Add to that the fact that we all show up with built-in biases, "our own" way of doing things, and more than a bit of selfishness, you have the perfect environment for conflict, misunderstanding, and/or fractured relationships. In addition, outside influences, family problems, and personal issues put pressure on organizational relationships. Not long ago, school closures forced families with two working parents to make very difficult, highly emotional choices. Which parent would stay home with the children and become their teacher, and which would go to work? These types of disruptions to our schedules, rhythms of life, and even sleep patterns can impact how well we work with others.

For all the above reasons, it can be a challenge to get everyone to pull together.

The solution? Team building. Relationship development. Getting all team members on the same page. This happens when everyone has the skill and will to create and maintain productive relationships with others. In organizations today, this is not an option, it is a necessity.

Relationships at Risk

In my experience, relationships that breakdown do not get better over time, instead, they get worse. This phenomenon is seen all around us. Couples that pledge their undying love for each other end up in divorce court a year later seeking to destroy the former love of their lives. Family members that once were close suffer through icy holiday dinners because of disagreements over politics or who gets Aunt Gertie's favorite potholders when she passes. Neighbors no longer speak to each other because of disagreements about how short to cut the grass. On it goes.

This tendency for relational break down naturally carries over into the world of work and other team settings. When this happens, the collapse of individual relationships is only the beginning of the problems. Soon, communication shuts down, cooperation disappears, productivity and quality suffer, and the mission is in jeopardy. Like a highly contagious disease, relational failure spreads throughout the organization lowering morale, employee engagement, and customer experience. The resiliency that was once so evident, now fades as personal agendas, wounded pride, indignation, and a host of other self-oriented emotions override commitment to the whole. Without an antidote, the team is in serious trouble. So, since it is obvious that the team is not working well together, is it time to dive into some sort of team building program? Not quite yet... in existing organizations, it would first be wise to determine what caused the breakdown and to understand why team members are no longer demonstrating the core values.

A good way to gain an understanding of the genesis of the problem is to conduct a survey of either the most impacted areas or the entire organization. If the issue is more localized, then I recommend an intervention whereby a professional facilitator meets with members of that group and allows them to voice the concerns that caused the break in relationships.

Over the years, I learned that a team building program cannot make up for the lack of a clear mission, goals, and values, undefined leadership expectations, low quality products or services, and a host of other things. No amount of training can compensate for deficiencies in these other areas. However, when an organization has the basics in place, and it discovers that the cause of the relational breakdown is either a general lack of respect for others or that the team members do not understand how to demonstrate team behaviors, then it is time for a team building effort.

Team Building: How It Is Done

We should make no mistake that, for many people, cooperation with others is not natural. It is a foreign act that must be taught and reinforced continually after any initial training has been completed. Team building was, is, and always will be a complex undertaking. It should empower members of an organization to do two things: work together to accomplish the organization's mission, and understand how to demonstrate its core values during interactions with others. Unless a team building program is designed and presented in a manner that accomplishes both tasks, it will fail to provide much real benefit. Also, true team building takes place when *groups* of people learn to work more effectively together, not when a few enlightened people begin talking about it.

The basis for any team building activities must be found in the organization's mission, core values, and operating principles. As with any leadership development activity, team building cannot be a theoretical program that someone, either internally or externally, dreamed up. Instead, it must be part of the organization's effort to help all staff members live out their commitment to its mission and values.

After providing team training to tens of thousands of staff members around the globe, I conclude that the most effective teams possess the following qualities and conditions.

- Clear purpose and direction
- Effective leadership

- Productive interpersonal relations
- Communication/listening skills
- Problem solving, decision making, and planning skills
- Trust-based relationships
- Productive methods of conflict resolution
- Proper technical skills, knowledge, and abilities
- Sufficient resources, information, supplies, and equipment
- Fair performance evaluation, recognition, and reward systems

Leaders can use the above list to conduct a mental survey of their team[s]. Whether the entire organization, smaller departments, groups of leaders, or some other subsection, the qualities above will have a significant impact on the team's performance.

We Need Each Other

Here is a simple truth: In most cases, people working in effective teams accomplish more than an equal or even greater number of people working individually. True teamwork produces benefits in both productivity and personal satisfaction, regardless of which type of organization you are part of.

Years ago, I heard one man's account of heaven and hell. He described hell as a banquet hall filled with millions of people. They were seated across from one another at tables covered with the most scrumptious food imaginable. Tantalizing sights and tempting aromas filled the hall. However, there was one problem. The handles on the eating utensils were four feet long and could only be grasped at the very end. This made it virtually impossible for people to feed themselves. They could not get the food into their mouths.

Their frustrations soon grew into anger and rage that lasted throughout all eternity. Then, the man described heaven. At first glance, heaven seemed similar in every respect to the warmer place to the south ... The same type of banquet hall, the same wonderful food, and the same long-handled utensils that could be grasped only at the very end. However, the people at the heavenly banquet tables were content. Instead of angry cries, laughter filled the hall. Close inspection showed the reason for their joy. Rather than trying to serve themselves, the people used their utensils to serve someone across the table, who would then return the kindness.

This story will never win a theological debate, but it does make the point about teamwork. We get more accomplished when we work together and when we look for ways to serve those around us. We need each other.

HEART CRY INTERNATIONAL

An interview with Carla Ives, founder of Heart Cry International

C arla Ives founded Heart Cry International in 1991, housed in a tiny office at a church parsonage in Mount Pleasant, Michigan. Her vision was to train, equip, and resource national pastors, leaders, teachers, and parents to teach the next generation to know and follow Jesus; to disciple them into the wholeness and healing that salvation brings.

She was moved with compassion for the countless at-risk youth around the world that were being abused, exploited, trafficked, and literally destroyed.

Since then, the organization has grown in size and scope. Their training seminars have hosted thousands of attendees at times. Also, they have impacted 45 nations with training, materials and/or resources. They now have Child Sponsorship Programs operating in Sri Lanka, Kenya, Uganda, Nigeria, Brazil, and Haiti. In addition, they operate a Child Feed fund distributed to ministry partners in 16 countries.

Question: What were your greatest challenges?

Carla: Me. My heart being bigger than my pocketbook. Wrong belief systems based on wrong teaching I'd received early in ministry that led to decisions bringing debt and stress on both my family and ministry. I've since learned to slow down, wait for God to reveal the full plan and only **do what He provides for**. It hurts my heart at times still to say "no" to a genuine, painful need. However, I've learned to pray and trust God to provide through others when I cannot help.

Also, being a woman in a man's world—30 years ago a pastor's wife played the piano and taught Sunday School. She didn't travel the world alone, preaching and teaching without access to a cell phone.

Question: When times got tough, how did the concept of resilience play a part in your continued success?

Carla: I've experienced different versions of "tough" in the 40 years I've been in ministry. I've been physically assaulted, threatened, and almost thrown in jail when I ministered in restricted parts of the world. I've been publicly belittled because of my gender. I've had to be away from my family and know what it is to cry myself to sleep at night.

The toughest times were when I failed. I don't think there is anything more painful than telling a houseful of street boys that you don't have the money to keep the home going anymore or telling children in an orphanage you have to send them to someone else's orphanage because you can't pay for the staff or house anymore. It was tough when friends turned away, feeling I lacked faith or let the children down. If ever I considered quitting, it was then. But ... I couldn't shut off the fire of love that burned in my heart for the children of the world. When I closed my eyes, I saw their faces. Today, I'm so glad I didn't quit!

Question: What are you most proud of?

Carla: I'm proud I didn't give up when it was hard. Proud and incredibly thankful. I wouldn't miss this sweet and fruitful season of ministry for anything in the world. It was worth what it took to persevere.

Question: Was there a time when your team needed to be revised, transformed, or rebuilt? Explain.

Carla: This question honestly made me laugh! In this type of work, you are constantly revising. Every country requires a tweaking of the materials, training and presentation based on what will work in that culture and situation. I have seven translation projects going this week. I'm rewriting our Multi-Generational Discipleship Institute course for the third time. Things like the pandemic of 2020 and other natural disasters demand a shift in the way we do things.

When I first started our organization, I called it Reach the Children. Eight years later, we weren't just teaching children, but we were also expanding to train national leaders in areas of high exploitation and abuse. One community in Brazil had 90% of their children and teens already abused by generational incest and sex-trafficking. Ultimately, we decided to change the name to Heart Cry International.

Question: **Have you done any training, development, or coaching for your leaders or staff? If so, what did you do and what was the impact?**

We've done many different things over the year. We've brought in speakers to train and specialists in areas we wanted to improve. I do bi-monthly on-line meetings with my overseas team and use a portion of the time for training, encouragement and listening to them. The more I focus on equipping the team, the stronger the ministry becomes!

Question: What advice do you have for anyone wanting to either launch a new organization or to revitalize an existing one?

Carla: Don't be in a hurry. Make sure you have weighed the cost for you and your family before you begin. Wait until you have the first steps nailed down, the funds to get started and to carry you for at least a few years ahead. Though your vision may be large, take small steps. Build your team. Establish a foundation that will hold up as your work expands.

Take care of *you* in the process. You are more than the work you do. If you do not have the funds to do something, wait. Work waits. If you miss an opportunity there will be others. Enjoy the journey!

CHAPTER 15

SOLVING PROBLEMS TOGETHER

I t is time for a quick review. By this point in the process, many great things have happened for your team and/or the entire organization. If you have followed the process, here are the major milestones:

- You have **established your purpose and direction** with a new vision, mission, and core strategies.

- You have **organized your work** by setting goals, projects, and assigned individual tasks. You have established your measures of success.

- You have **created your culture** by developing core values, as well as establishing clear leadership expectations.

- You have begun the process of **developing your people** by providing leadership training and coaching, and you are helping team members build and maintain strong interpersonal relationships.

So, everything is perfect, and your success is guaranteed, right? Well, not quite yet. No matter how clear the mission, how sound the values, how effective the leaders or how cooperative the staff, an organization always runs into problems. Something breaks; a shipment is late; internal communication collapses; a new competitor emerges; a pandemic hits, and countless other problems spring up. When these occur, a swift and professional response is needed. In the old days, that meant that a few top people in the organization roll up their sleeves and attempt to fix what is wrong. Today there is a better way. Solving problems together.

The Problem with Problems

Problems are normal, natural, and can even be construc-
tive if addressed properly. The key is to have all members
of the organization ready, willing, and able to participate
in problem solving whenever needed. Problems must
be solved *as* they arise to keep the organization moving
ahead. The only rational approach is to train people
at all levels, so that they understand their authority,
boundaries, and which resources are available to them.
An organization's effectiveness accelerates exponentially
once its members have mastered problem-solving and
are authorized to use their skills within their own areas
of responsibility.

There is a lot of truth to the old saying: "Two heads
are better than one." The modern term for this concept
is *synergy*, which means that one plus one is *greater* than
two. From an organizational perspective, when two or
more people combine their insights about a problem,
then the solution is likely to be better than if they had
analyzed it separately. In some instances, the solution
may not necessarily be better; however, it may have been
discovered more swiftly. As a final benefit of cooperative

problem-solving efforts, the solution will have more support during the implementation phase because of the collective effort.

I have seen countless "problem solving sessions" that produced zero results. The reasons vary and include poor interpersonal relationships within the group, but even more common is the lack of an agreed upon process to analyze the situation. Some start looking for solutions, others want to find causes, still others begin to philosophize about why there are so many problems in the world. In these environments, no causes are found, no solutions are implemented, and nerves fray.

Fortunately, I have also seen trained groups of problem solvers discover millions of dollars in cost savings, streamline work processes, and create new approaches to customer service. I need to underscore the fact that the people involved were professionally trained. Problem solving efforts succeed *only* when the individuals involved are properly prepared, meaning that their interpersonal relationships are solid, no hidden agendas exist, and when they employ a common approach during problem-solving sessions. The basic terminology and sequence of problem-solving steps can be learned quickly and used for a lifetime.

Solve One and Cause Another

Problem solving training should help people develop a logical, systematic approach to problem analysis. Once this approach has been mastered, it can be applied to any situation in that person's professional or personal life. In many instances, the understanding of a systematic problem-solving process is just as valuable as having detailed knowledge about a particular product or work process. Without a common process to approach problems, it is easy to "solve" one problem that causes another.

I recall a wealthy gentleman living in a northern climate that did just that. It seems that he had grown tired of shoveling snow off his sidewalk each winter and planned to solve this problem permanently. His solution was simple: he installed heating pipes under his concrete driveway and sidewalks. The pipes would warm the cement during the winter, melting any snow that dared fall on his domain.

When the first heavy snowfall came, he excitedly turned on his heating system and waited for the results. His system worked to perfection; his was the only sidewalk in the neighborhood to remain free of snow. The man went to sleep confident that his neighbors soon would flock to his property to marvel at his invention. The next morning, he awoke to find that he was half right in his prediction. It seems that his neighbors' *dogs* found his snow-free sidewalks an ideal place to relieve themselves. Evidently, the canines found the warm surface a welcome change from the cold, high snowdrifts to which they had grown accustomed. His four-legged neighbors liked this innovation so much that they came to show their appreciation daily.

That winter, the gentleman problem-solver had more to shovel than just snow.

Everyone is a Problem Solver

I am a firm believer in the notion that *every* person is an expert in his or her field, position, area, or job. Individual superstars rarely win championships—it takes every member of a team to bring about success. Often, innovation and invention come from ordinary people with extraordinary insight. All it requires is for leaders to invest in the training of the company's members and then give them opportunities to use their newfound skills. In this type of environment, problems are quickly addressed and resolved by the people closest to the situation.

Organizations that utilize their human resources this way soon experience a wonderful transition from problem solving, to problem prevention, and finally, to capitalizing on innovative competitive opportunities. In these dynamic environments, team members are willing and able to anticipate problems, improve existing processes, and to suggest new products and services. This results in an organization that can quickly adjust to any critical issue and to seize upon emergent opportunities, even before the competition knows they exist.

Learning the Process

In recent decades, many companies tried to implement programs aimed at solving and preventing problems related to productivity, profitability, and/or product quality. These programs have been called by different names such as Statistical Process Control, Six Sigma, Quality Improvement Programs, Process Improvement, LEAN, and numerous others. Some of these programs produce good results; others fail miserably for predictable reasons.

Just learning a few tools such as Pareto Charts, Histograms, and Fish Bone Diagrams does not teach the systematic thinking required to be an effective problem solver. Sadly, some organizations that attempted to teach a form of systematic problem solving made their programs overly complex which caused them to be rejected by busy team members that only wanted to be more effective at their work.

This meant that staff members sat through one- or two-day training sessions, wrestling with unfamiliar terms rather than learning to think systematically about problems. Once they returned to work, they realized that little was retained, so there was not much return on the investment for either the individuals or the organization. All that was, is, and will be needed is for team members to share an easy to understand, step by step process, that is taught using familiar language.

After seeing so many companies struggle with this, I made the commitment to design a training course that would be easy to learn and apply. The result was the seven-step problem-solving process below that has since been used by countless organizations for several decades.

The goal of this process is twofold. First, I wanted to teach people to think rationally, logically, and sequentially when facing problems. Second, I sought to empower people with a common approach and easy to understand terms in problem solving sessions. Here are the steps in the process that I call Team Problem Solving®.

Step 1: Identify the Problems

Step 2: Prioritize the Problems

Step 3: Identify Probable Causes

Step 4: Confirm Actual Cause

Step 5: Set Solution Goals

Step 6: Decide on a Solution

Step 7: Develop an Action Plan

Once people are trained in the above process, there are multiple ways for them to use their skills to support their organization. First, individuals can simply analyze the problems they face in their work area. Second is when a problem impacts more than one person or area, then several team members can come together informally to analyze, locate the cause, evaluate solution options, and then implement the solution. The third option is when a problem is systemic and needs more attention to solve it. When this happens, a multi-disciplinary team can be assembled and given the time, information, and freedom to solve the problem.

Problem Solving Leads to Innovation

Once the members of your team are skilled at solving existing problems, they turn their attention to the future. When this happens, they use their insight to prevent problems from occurring and they begin to identify innovations to propel the organization forward. The innovation process is much the same as the problem-solving process in that success depends on finding causes or changes. Instead of asking "what caused the breakdown of the equipment," the question becomes "what could bring about an increase in sales or customer satisfaction, etc.?"

When staff members are trained in the full process of problem solving, they serve as a protective shield over the organization. Problems come, but staff, at all levels, are willing and able to address them quickly and professionally.

Just for Fun

Mature professionals recognize that problems are part of organizational life and take them head-on. Others struggle with the very mention of the word *problem*.

I saw this firsthand at a manufacturing company whose general manager was frustrated by his subordinates' constant griping about problems. One day, the executive decided to put a stop to it by instructing his team to never again bring the term "problem" into their staff meetings. Instead, they were only to bring the term "opportunities" for discussion and resolution.

This worked well until one day a flustered young manager entered the meeting more than an hour late. His shirt was torn, there was grease on his face, and sweat poured off his brow. His appearance and late arrival shocked those in attendance into a stunned silence. Finally, the general manager asked the question on everyone's mind. "What happened to you?"

Mindful of the mandate never to mention the word *problem* again, the frustrated manager tried several times to recount his story only to stop mid-sentence. Red cheeks glowing with frustration, he finally blurted out: "Well boss, I just came across an "opportunity" on the shop floor that I think is going to *put us out of business!*"

Yes . . . that really happened.

CHAPTER 16

MAKING WORK-FROM-HOME WORK

The mindset of today's workforce is unquestionably different from what it was just a generation ago. No longer are employees, at any level, content to apply for a job, wait for an affirmative phone call from an HR department staff member and then sign up for 30 years of service before receiving a gold watch and monthly pension check. These days, pension checks are mighty rare (and very few wear watches anymore).

In today's seller's market, employees are more selective on which jobs they will accept. They also change jobs at the speed of light, creating immense challenges for organizations. The obvious solution is to hire the best people available and then keep them, but that is much easier said than done.

Company leaders are employing various retention strategies such as signing bonuses, increased PTO, more rapid progression to higher levels of responsibility, and all sorts of social events in hopes of creating friendships among the troops. But are any of these having the desired impact on a large scale?

One of my Executive Associates, Steven D. Molitor, did extensive research on this subject for his master's degree thesis and discovered some fascinating information. Following are some highlights of his research.

One of the more effective changes organizations are implementing seeks to address two relatively new conditions within the workforce: **two working parents** and the increasing desire on the part of employees for **greater flexibility and personal freedom.**

To address this new paradigm, many organizations have implemented work-from-home (WFH) policies. Some of these are successful, and others are simply not.

Based on Steven Molitor's research, here are the seven keys to success for any company interested in implementing a flexible, sustainable work-from-home policy:

Technology

The technology used to connect leaders and staff must be professional, up-to-date, and compatible. This includes computers, modems, software, cell phones, and the proper programs used for connection, whether Zoom, Skype, Teams, and/or any new options that come out in the future. Proper use of cameras and volume control are two related essentials.

General Expectations

All expectations must be made clear in terms of performance metrics, time, meetings, and more. Any assumptions made by either party will result in significant misunderstandings and the joys of flexibility will be overshadowed by confusion. Items in this category include how much time is expected to be spent 'working', when times of scheduled connections such as virtual staff meetings are to occur, and/or whether one-on-one meetings between leaders and staff members are implemented. In addition, assignments given must come with detailed performance standards, be assigned a priority, and include timelines for completion.

Another important aspect of these expectations deals with personal and family needs. If a staff member is caring for their school-age children or elderly parents, they will likely need some degree of flexibility when it comes to their work. Remember, it is not the number of hours spent that matter, but rather the accomplishment of agreed-upon goals, projects and tasks. This requires a paradigm shift for many leaders who historically measured performance by what time a worker showed up and what time they left work.

Protocol and Proper Etiquette

In every organization, there will be expected standards of etiquette that need to be followed by all participants. This could include dress code for online meetings, when and when not to mute one's microphone, how to 'raise one's hand' during group sessions to prevent interruptions, and more. The internet is filled with embarrassing videos of staff members who thought they were muted . . . but weren't. Others forgot to turn off their cameras and were caught severely underdressed. Amusing for a wider audience, but not so much for the individuals involved.

I recently had to help a company work through a snafu where a subordinate forgot to mute his microphone following a heated exchange with his supervisor. Using off-color language and veiled threats, the employee blurted out his displeasure with leadership and his tirade was heard by the entire management team. It did not go well for that gentleman.

Working from home does not cancel out an organization's mission or dilute its values. Staff members are to focus their efforts properly and live according to the stated values just as if they still reported to an office.

Personal Connection

Leaders with staff working from home must make it a priority to remain connected relationally with each staff member. Failure to do so relegates the supervisor to a simple monitor of outcomes as opposed to an effective leader.

This personal connection requires a great deal of interaction between leaders and those working under his or her care. Ideally, this happens both in person and via electronic means. Whenever possible, leaders should set up face-to-face gatherings for those working from home to ensure that bonds are built not only with the leader, but also with other team members.

The connection must be both caring and consistent. A quarterly or even monthly check-in is not sufficient to maintain or build a productive relationship. When leaders interact with staff, it is good to have a checklist of items to discuss until or unless it becomes second nature. The list could include personal and family well-being, progress on established goals, any changes that have occurred since the last discussion, identification of any roadblocks that the staff person had encountered, as well as time for mentoring and thanks for the staff member's efforts.

Trust and Verification

Years ago, former president Ronald Reagan was asked about his approach to foreign relations. He is quoted as saying, "Trust . . . but verify." That's great advice for leaders with staff members working offsite. Another way to view this is from the paradigm of a juror who must enter deliberations with an 'innocent unless proven guilty' mindset.

Employees that work from home need to be treated as trusted members of the organization, as opposed to bandits who have been waiting to rip off the company for a few extra hours of free pay. This is no different from having employees working in cubicles for eight hours each day—a leader never *really* knows who is working effectively and who isn't. It has never mattered where someone sat, or stood, for a finite amount of time; the real payoff is what they accomplished during that time.

The beauty of having staff work from home is that a leader can increase the clarity of expectations and monitor outcomes very easily, provided those expectations are clear to begin with.

Specific Expectations and Assignments

Leaders who succeed in overseeing staff working from home ensure that each member of the team understands his or her goals, priorities, timelines, deliverables, milestones, and quality metrics of all projects. In addition, the relationship expectation between and among team members must also be covered in detail very early in the process as new work arrangements are implemented.

Celebration

Whether staff members work inside a cramped office or at a table in their bedroom, there will always be a need for celebration of effort and accomplishment. This is especially true for employees that do repetitive work as they benefit from encouraging words and acts even more than those doing higher level tasks.

These celebrations and affirmations may take place during monthly in-person gatherings, or they may happen during online staff meetings. Regardless of where and how they occur, celebrations are a powerful way to let staff know that while they may be out of sight, they are not out of mind.

Work-from-home is here to stay and, if properly handled, will continue to provide benefits to organizations, families and individuals staff members alike.

CHAPTER 17

CHECK-IN, CHECK-UP

Y ou have two fundamental ways to know if all is well within your organization. First, you can wait until trouble shows up at your door as evidenced by angry, disgruntled team members, complaining customers, missed assignments, financial problems, and a host of other negative issues. My guess is that is not the preferred way. Second, you can regularly conduct assessment surveys of the people connected to your organization. This may include your leadership group, staff members, your volunteers, customers, or even community members that may have some input about your organization.

It is important to obtain the full picture of issues to prevent undue focus on symptoms rather than actual causes. By this, I mean that one individual brings a defective part into a manufacturing meeting and declares that *quality* is the problem. Another brings in a customer complaint and is certain that *customer service* is where to invest the company's resources. Still another overhears two employees arguing in the hallway and states emphatically that their problem is a lack of *teamwork*.

The impact of these different perceptions can be profound. Why? Because the way you define a problem dictates how you solve it. The organization may invest hundreds of thousands of dollars to "fix" product quality, customer service, or broken relationships without ever confirming that these issues are the ones creating the greatest threat to the team.

A careful assessment can reveal the entire picture, and provide direction for resource allocation, as well as any needed tweaks to the core strategies or goals.

The concepts of assessing and evaluating are certainly not foreign to most organizations. Many regularly perform audits of their finances, keep track of inventory, and have near instant access to performance in productivity, quality, turnover and other indicators. No one would challenge the wisdom of such practices. However, if it makes sense to assess these signs of organizational health, then it makes even more sense to regularly assess the condition of the organization's culture.

Organizational assessment surveys may be called by different names including employee surveys, morale surveys, cultural surveys, employee engagement surveys, and others. Regardless of what they are called, the goal is:

- To obtain perceptions of strengths and weaknesses of the organization's culture from the staff at all levels.

- To compile and present the survey results in a way that leaders can understand and act upon them.

- To involve all members of the organization in the process of change. (Remember, meaningful involvement = Support and Commitment)

- To let the staff know the survey results and to communicate what the organization intends to do to address any deficiencies identified during the process.

Whether yours is a new organization or one that has been in existence for years, chances are that the assessment survey will show room for improvement. Therefore, it takes courage and maturity on the part of the leaders who commission the survey to risk hearing some criticism.

Cultural Survey Options

An assessment may be approached in various ways, each having pluses and minuses. For instance, data may be collected from the entire organization or from a smaller representative sample, such as focus groups. Also, the assessment may utilize numerical data from a computerized survey, or it may use more subjective data from face-to-face interviews. It is ideal to use a combination of the two, whereby you gather numerical data and then follow up with face-to-face interviews to learn the intricacies of people's perceptions. I use the term "perceptions" because whatever someone perceives to be true becomes truth to him or her. Perceptions are then acted upon as if true... even if they are not.

Through the years, my associates and I have interviewed tens of thousands of people using a systematic face-to-face approach that gathers information from nearly 100 percent of an organization's members. This is time-consuming and tedious, but once completed, this process provides more of an x-ray than a snapshot of what is truly happening inside the organization.

The Blind Men and the Elephant

A proper assessment gathers input from all levels of the organization and then combines the data to show a complete picture of what is happening. Is it necessary to go through so much hassle just to find out what people think? Can't leaders just figure it out? Unfortunately, no, they cannot. It is much like the parable of the blind men who attempt to describe an elephant by touching it in different spots. One man touches the elephant's side and describes it as a wall. Another touches its trunk and describes it as a snake. Still another man touches the elephant's leg and describes it as a tree. Each is firmly convinced that he has a complete understanding of elephants.

Countless times, I have seen this story played out in the corporate world by modern-day blind men and women who sincerely believed that because they are in positions of leadership, they somehow "know" the intricacies of the organization, when they only know a small part of the whole.

The Hidden Benefits of an Assessment Survey

There is more to a properly performed assessment than just gathering data about your organization. I have found that assessments not only uncover the real strengths and weaknesses of an organization but also can unify and prepare people for change. I believe that at least 50 percent of the value gained from an assessment comes from the fact that each person involved develops *ownership* in the change process. They know that their input will be used to change direction or to stay the current course if all is well, and it is human nature to want to influence direction and destiny.

It is important to remember two things about assessments: First, people feel ownership for what they help build. Second, people take care of what they own. Therefore, meaningful involvement in a survey increases the sense of ownership in the change process. For this reason, it is wise to involve as many people as possible.

Assessment Topics

The following are topics I often use to customize questions asked during cultural surveys for business, government, healthcare, nonprofits, and other types of organizations. They are listed in no specific order.

- Mission
- Critical issues and competitive opportunities
- Core values
- Trust and openness
- Leader effectiveness
- Communication and listening skills
- Information flow
- Interdependence
- Morale and engagement
- Positive reinforcement
- Corrective feedback

- Performance improvement

- Approach to problem solving

During the design process, I always leave room for leaders to add specific questions that matter to them. They may want feedback on some new initiative, some external situation that has impacted the organization such as the COVID crisis of 2020, or how staff is responding to new government regulations impacting their industry.

The Assessment Is Finished. Now What?

An assessment is one step in the cultural change process, not the end of it.

Once the survey data is collected, there are still two important steps to be completed.

First, the results must be studied by the organization's leaders. This process may take two to three weeks for them to digest, sort out, and prepare responses to the issues.

Second, the results and basic steps that will be taken to address any issues raised are then communicated to staff members. This is particularly important. Short-sighted leaders leave this step out which results in low credibility and even lower morale for the staff that contributed to the survey. Remember, the staff know the issues already, they just want to know they have been heard and that their leaders are prepared to act upon the information that was gathered.

Feedback Methods and Lessons Learned

Leaders *must* accept the survey results with an open mind. If the data is critical of the organization or its leadership, resentment too often is the primary reaction. None of us like to have our shortcomings, real or perceived, exposed. It helps to know that staff or volunteers did not identify problems to hurt anyone's feelings. Instead, they did so to help the organization become its best. An immature or overly defensive response from leaders can do further damage to their credibility. Remember, a proper assessment is designed to focus on future change, not past blame.

Not only should the information gathered during an assessment be fed back to everyone who participated in the interviews, but whenever possible, it should be done in person, not through email, memos, or bulletins, which are often misinterpreted.

Keys to a successful feedback session:

1. Leaders should never minimize, place blame [except upon themselves if appropriate], or make excuses for any shortcomings exposed in the assessment. Excuses are not reasons. Excuses do not create positive change; only plans of action do.

2. Leaders should not promise that all problems will be *solved* within a short period. That is unrealistic. Staff members just need to know that the issues will be dealt with in a reasonable amount of time.

3. Leaders should talk about new opportunities identified during the survey. These may include new product lines, new services, and/or other innovations.

4. Finally, leaders should be prepared to explain any misunderstandings the assessment identifies. In my experience, from 20 to 40 percent of the

problems identified during an assessment are a result of misperception, miscommunication, and misunderstanding. These are easily reconciled with proper explanation, which gives an immediate morale boost to the organization.

The Blueprint for Change

Once a survey has been completed, things get exciting. Some problems are identified and will be solved, and some new opportunities come to light and can be added to the team's strategies or goals. The credibility of leadership grows as staff responds to the transparent sharing of the good, bad, and even the ugly.

The survey results provide a clear blueprint for change and increases the team's resiliency due to the increased trust gained in the process. The stage is once again set for ongoing success.

SUCCESS STORY:
BEAR VIDEO PRODUCTIONS

An interview with Cody "Bear" Knott, founder and owner of Bear Productions

Bear Productions, located in Grand Rapids, Michigan, officially became an LLC in 2016. The organization was created to produce innovative video projects for a variety of clients. This includes couples wanting a dream wedding video to be cherished for a lifetime, local and national companies seeking cutting edge, captivating videos to set them apart from their competitors, as well as creative videos for non-profit organizations to help them tell their compelling stories.

The founder, Cody Knott, learned the business working with other companies and production houses before launching out on his own. He worked on local, national, and international productions, such as *Jeni: Seeking the Extraordinary* and *TV4DADS*, that air throughout the world.

Bear Productions went the way of many start up organizations and lost money in its first year. However, since then, the organization has nearly doubled in projects and revenue each year. As the production schedule has increased, Bear Productions has been able to provide subcontract work for five other professionals.

Question: What were your greatest challenges to success?

Cody: One of my greatest challenges to success are staying motivated as I generally work from home. I'm not proud to admit that there were times my pillow or favorite TV show took precedence over my business. My second greatest challenge is caring too much about what other people think. By this, I mean that I want to thrill my customers, but at times I can "give" too much and end up losing financially. I've definitely grown in this area, but there still needs to be a lot of improvement.

Question: **When times got tough, how did the concept of resilience play a part in your continued success?**

Cody: I sought out mentors in my field to learn what they did when things got hard. I watched a lot of YouTube videos of production companies that motivated me and to keep my mind fresh and up to date with new filming techniques. I am really good with people, so when times were hard, I would go to networking events and get my company name out there.

Question: **What are you most proud of?**

Cody: I am most proud of my company's financial growth over the last four years. I started with absolutely nothing . . . except debt. Now, the company has solid revenue that I hope will continue to grow. To add to that, my own personal growth as a business owner. I can confidently quote projects accurately now without undue stress that I'll over or under charge. Also, I can have tough business conversations with my clients instead of being passive or shying away. Paperwork and taxes still feel daunting at times, but I'm able to muscle through it knowing it is what needs to be done in order for my business to run and to be able to do what I love to do.

Question: Was there a time when your team needed to be revised, transformed, or rebuilt? Explain.

Cody: Absolutely. It's important to me to have a strong marketing image that people gravitate to and remember. So, I changed my logo and the look of my company a handful of times. I've finally reached a point that works, and people are remember my company. Also, I've had to upgrade my equipment almost every year in order to stay relevant and competitive. I have restructured how I quote my clients more times than I can count. I needed to make sure that how I was quoting my clients was fair, competitive, worth my time, and consistent.

Question: Have you done any training, development, or coaching for your leaders or staff? If so, what did you do and what was the impact?

Cody: I've trained many subcontractors that have come onto production shoots with me. Whether that was running a camera, making sure they knew the correct settings and composition of shots I was looking for, setting up 3-point lighting during interviews, drone operating, gimbal operating, or even the best way to communicate with my clients. After doing that a couple of times I was able to build full trust that my contractors would do the right thing, execute tasks well, and represent my business well. We would show up on set, greet each other, and get to work. It was really nice.

Question: What advice do you have for anyone wanting to either launch a new organization or to grow an existing one?

Cody: Find mentors who have at least 5+ years of experience owning and running a successful business and pick their brains about everything. I wish I would have done that sooner before I started my business, but it is crucial to have those people in your life to not only give some knowledge but also to push and motivate you.

CHAPTER 18

YOUR BEST INVESTMENT:

TRAINING AND DEVELOPMENT

W hether your organization has existed for more than a century, or you just recently opened your doors, where is the best place to invest your hard-earned money? Upgraded equipment? Newest technology? Marketing campaign? Social media platforms? Any of these might be a good option, but the wisest investment may well be directly into your team members.

It is said that *people are an organization's most valuable resource.* While this is generally true, there needs to be a couple of additions to that statement. The following is more accurate: *People are an organization's most valuable resource . . . when they are committed to the mission and values, and when they are equipped to do the tasks assigned to them.*

Not every person that joins an organization walks in on day one, fully prepared to perform at the highest level. They may shine in an interview, but all they bring with them are their experiences, education, and insights learned through life up to that moment, which may or may not be sufficient to succeed in their new roles. Training and development make up any gaps and prepare your people for success and also is key to maintaining the organization's desired culture.

Return on Investment

In the year 2021, corporate America invested over **$92,000,000,000 in training and development** of its human resources. While some of this investment *may* have come from corporate benevolence, much of it comes from the same motivation that drives investments in infrastructure, equipment, and technology . . . to get a return. The beauty of this investment in team members is it provides the ultimate win/win scenario.

The "win" for the organization that finances education, training, and development of its people comes in many forms including:

- Greater productivity
- More profitability
- Higher quality
- Reduced turnover
- Increased employee engagement

Fortunately, properly devised education and training activities are also a "win" for team members as well. Recently, the Gallup Organization released a survey that showed some interesting facts about employee engagement, job satisfaction, and retention. It indicated that eighty-four percent of employees who received at least six days of training within the previous year said they were satisfied with their jobs, compared to only seventy percent of those who received no job training.

In addition, eighty percent of the people surveyed said that the availability of company-sponsored training programs was a factor in deciding whether to accept a new job with another organization or to remain in their current positions.

Despite the statistics and success stories of organizations that have invested in their people, there are still many leaders today that gladly spend millions of dollars on new technology or equipment, but balk at spending a comparatively small amount on employee training and development. This makes little sense.

The goal of workforce development is quite basic. It is to equip people with the relevant information, knowledge, and skills necessary to be productively involved in the accomplishment of the mission, in ways that are consistent with core values. In today's world, education and training are no longer options; they are necessities. Just as no organization can afford to allow its technology or equipment to become obsolete, neither can it allow its human resources to become outdated or feel unappreciated. To be clear, this has nothing to do with the age of employees. Any organization whose strategy is "out with the old and in with the new" is making a huge mistake. The 'old' are full of experience, wisdom, and insights that can be transferred to the 'new' in mentoring relationships. Regardless of their age, we must continually upgrade each employee's skills, knowledge, awareness of new technology, and emotional intelligence.

Preventive Maintenance for Your Human Resources

In recent decades, a shift has taken place concerning maintenance of machines and other equipment. Gone is the old practice of running equipment until it completely breaks down. This destructive method has been replaced by preventive policies that initially seem counterintuitive. The pioneers of this practice faced stiff opposition from doubters. Shut down equipment that is running properly? Can that possibly make sense? The answer is yes. It makes infinitely better sense to invest time performing minor repairs, upgrading technology, and maintaining equipment at regular intervals, even when things were running properly, than to mindlessly wait for random, perhaps irreparable breakdowns to occur at the worst possible times.

We need a similar mindset change concerning our human resources. Just like equipment, our human resources can "break" at the worst time, leaving an organization to flounder. I recall a pilot strike that occurred in the late 1990s that cost one airline more than two-hundred million dollars. I guarantee that some preventive maintenance performed on the relationships between management and the pilots *before* the strike would have saved them a huge amount of money, time, and energy.

To achieve this new mindset, you first must realize that money spent on employee education and training represents a wise investment rather than just another cost. People are the only resource that has the capacity to think, reason, innovate, problem-solve, and plan. They can adapt, they can adjust, and they can figure out solutions to problems that do not yet exist. They are well worth the investment.

Organizations are often staffed by members of several different generations. Some may have joined during their late teen years, others when they were middle-aged and still others at the tail end of their careers. Regardless of when they arrived, they will either be a most valuable asset . . . or something less, and often the determining factor is the amount of education, training, and development they receive.

The Toolbox

Human resource training and development is accomplished by a variety of methods. These include:

- Workshops
- Training seminars
- 360 surveys
- Personal coaching
- Learning management systems
- Video-based learning

Buyer Beware

There is no shortage of companies offering generic training programs for organizations. Such programs provide general information about topics such as leadership or communication, however, they cannot possibly target the exact needs of the organization. Too many of these "one-day wonders" programs promise to teach everything there is to know about a complex subject in six hours or less . . . with coffee and donuts tossed in for good measure. In my experience, these can end up doing more harm than good.

I recall a warehouse manager who was facing a near rebellion from his staff. After interviewing his team, I discovered why they were so upset. The manager recently attended a one-day training seminar on pro-ductivity where he learned two new terms, *value-added* and *non-value added*. One day he literally told the members of his warehouse staff that that they added *no value* to the organization. This was an absurd misuse of the term, but he said it, nonetheless. Naturally, the employees were hurt, angry, and de-motivated by his insensitive and inaccurate comments. The manager did not intend to be offensive, he just learned enough about a subject to be dangerous to himself, his staff, and his organization.

This is not to say that some public seminars, even one day sessions, might not provide some value, how-ever, organizations have individual cultures and the one-size-fits-all approach to learning generally falls short of any developmental goal. There is a better way.

Foundations for Training and Development

Human resource development, whether training, coaching, counseling, or other forms, should always be based on an organization's mission, core values, and leadership expectations. These statements provide the foundation upon which all developmental activities must be based. Otherwise, we might as well just send everyone to the nearest one-day wonder and call it good.

Here is how it works. Organizational development professionals look at mission, values, and leadership expectations to identify the A, B, C's [Attitudes, Behaviors, and Communications] associated with each element of those guiding statements. Then, a plan is put in place to teach the appropriate behaviors to the members of the organization, whether at the leadership or staff level.

For example, if a leadership expectation is that of Productive Interpersonal Relationships, then a training session is created to teach the foundations of connecting with others, caring, and empathy. If a core value is that of Effective Communication, then a session is designed to teach the basics of two-way versus one-way communication, listening skills, public speaking and/or others.

Following the training sessions, the organization may schedule personal effectiveness surveys, personality profiles, 360 feedback, and/or coaching to help ensure that the team member has embraced the content and is applying it on the job.

Start at the Top

Every aspect of organizational growth and change begins with members of its leadership group. Occasionally, I get requests from leaders to help them transform their organizations, but they insist that only the lower-level staff need the help. I remember one company owner that requested that I go and "teach *those people* out there to be more productive." When I asked if they had done any developmental work with their supervisors, managers or executives, his reply was "we don't need that." I thanked him for the call and politely hung up ...

Development for executives and upper-level leaders often involves more coaching than training. This is because along the journey to the top, executives and top-level leaders likely have attended numerous training sessions and understand the *basics* of leadership, communication, strategic thinking, etc. However, knowing the basics and consistently applying those principles are two different things. Also, the higher one goes within an organization, the less likely they are to have anyone give them honest feedback on their performance . . . too risky. Coaching is a great way to help remove blind spots from top leaders so they can live the values and lead in ways that motivate others.

Four Elements of Successful Training and Development

Identify the Real Issue

Many times, I have been asked by organizational leaders to provide training in general subjects such as communications. When I ask why the training is needed, the response is often something like "because our people can't communicate with each other." My counter is

"Are you sure they *can't*, or perhaps they don't want to?" This leads to some deeper analysis of what is happening within the organization and typically the issue is more related to poor relationships or lack of trust, rather than an inability to communicate. Make sure the developmental activities target real needs. Information gathered during the cultural assessment can provide much-needed insight into real developmental needs.

No One-Day Wonders

Organizational transformation takes time and so does changing hearts and minds. Any developmental efforts should be planned out well in advance and have multiple opportunities to build new skills and shape the collective will of the people so that they align with the mission, values, and leadership expectations. Sending a few individuals off to be trained in anything other than technical subjects is more window dressing than serious development.

Make it Practical

People today are busy and have little time for theories, proven or unproven, when it comes to organizational development. My approach to training and development has always been to take complex subjects such as communication, relationships, teamwork, or leadership and convert them in simple, easy to apply concepts. This allows concepts to be learned quickly and implemented immediately, which was the point of the training in the first place.

Participative and Multi-Media Format, Not Lecture-Based

Today's leaders, staff, and volunteers want education and training that moves quickly, stimulates the mind with different media, and is highly participative. The old way of having an individual stand in front of a group droning on about a subject is sure to fail. Training must be a shared event, where everyone takes part.

The Three Foundations for Organizational Success

After many years in this field, I have distilled cultural training and development topics down to three major categories. When an organization focuses attention on these, there is little need for any additional "training" beyond job specific, technical or anything involving major changes in a person's work itself.

Foundation #1: Leadership

Foundation #2: Teambuilding

Foundation #3: Problem Solving

Of course, there are subsets in each category. For example, the topic of leadership includes vision, caring, communication, engagement techniques, etc. Teambuilding includes conflict resolution, communication, trust, decision making, etc. Problem Solving training encompasses a 7-step process, common terms used in the process, finding causes, identifying solution options, etc.

So, why the three primary categories? Because when an organization has people that can lead others, when its members can effectively work together as a team, and when all members can solve problems, make decisions, and establish plans, then there is little to stop that organization from succeeding.

The Future of Training and Development

In the future, the need for high quality training and development initiatives will increase. The reasons? They include stress, downsizing, pressure to perform, worldwide competition, global teams trying to work together, new technology, pandemics, political upheaval, and . . . did I mention stress? In the world of tomorrow, the technology, equipment, regulations, roles, and relationships will continue to do two things: change and increase in complexity. This requires that people be professionally educated and trained in a myriad of areas, or they and their organization will falter.

Remember, while we humans show signs of wear and tear as we age, we will never become obsolete. So, whether the development takes place in person, via a new internet-based platform, or using some other method, it will be essential for the organization's most valuable resources to remain proficient.

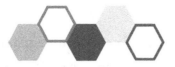

CHAPTER 19

MAKING IT LAST

A t this point in the journey, you are building your culture upon a solid mission and clear values, you have ongoing initiatives to develop the skills of your leaders and team members, and you regularly assess the performance, engagement levels, and overall condition of your organization. As a result, great things are happening and your human resources are productive, engaged, and committed. Now, we need to make sure that it lasts.

As we have already noted, a team's culture is based on a shared mission, clear core values, and consistent leadership expectations. Training and coaching sessions are great ways to help team members, at all levels, improve their skills so that they can live out and support these vital concepts. Fortunately, there are additional ways to help ensure that the progress made is sustained, literally becoming a way of life.

Interviewing and Hiring

Even before new team members step foot inside the organization, they can be exposed to the mission and values they will be expected to embrace. These statements are introduced to each potential employee or volunteer by your team's HR personnel or whoever is responsible for securing new talent. Once introduced, potential employees can be asked if they are supportive and willing to be committed to both the mission and values.

For those persons hired, the mission and values statements can be included in their employment package. When hiring a new supervisor, manager, executive, or administrator, a thorough explanation of the leadership expectations is also included at this phase. If the candidate enthusiastically embraces the concepts, that is a step in the right direction. However, if the response is tepid or worse, negative, then chances are good that the individual will fail as a leader.

Orientation and Onboarding

Once a person is hired or taken on as a volunteer, he or she must be given a proper orientation to the team, its mission, its core values, and a host of other issues. This may take place during sessions where new personnel learn about key issues of their employment. This orientation period is the perfect time to reinforce the importance of the team's mission and core values. It is important that new employee orientations don't become tests of endurance for excited staff members.

Not long ago, I was invited to help a large organization create a new approach to employee orientation, so I sat in the back of their auditorium to observe the current process. The next seven hours were painful as speaker after speaker addressed the assembly of new hires, droning on about his or her area of expertise. The new staff members sat in rows, facing the front, and had zero interaction with one another. Passionless presenters talked about parking, compliance, badges, security, and multiple programs that may or may not have been relevant to the new hires.

Mercifully, there was a 30-minute lunch break in the company cafeteria, which was followed by several more hours of lecture. At the end of the program, I asked one of the new staff members what he thought about the session. The young man grimaced and said, "I'm glad it's over."

In the weeks that followed, I worked with a small group of leaders from the organization to create a new experience for newly hired staff. We started fresh, literally with a blank 4 x 8-foot whiteboard. I asked them to identify those things that a new hire MUST know, learn, be exposed to before starting work. Not surprisingly, the list was quite short. There were some forms that had to be filled out, they needed to have a personal password to access the company computer system, and they needed to know where to park. All the other content had been added over the years without anyone ever asking why it was necessary. From there, we pondered how to make the new hires' experience more stimulating and memorable. To this end, we added in some video presentations on the company Mission and Values, and some team building exercises so the new staff could begin to build relationships with those around them.

One novel idea we came up with was a fifteen-question quiz that focused on unique aspects of the organization. We had the attendees form teams and gave small prizes to the team that got the most correct answers.

By approaching the new employee orientation this way, we were able to cut hours off the day, provide an exciting start to the new hires' careers, and to form lasting bonds within the workforce through the shared experience.

After an initial orientation, new team members need to experience an extended time of customized onboarding, where they learn the details of their new role, the location of their direct supervisor, how to find their work area, who to contact for which issues, and more. Again, the person providing the orientation can and should talk about the importance of the organization's culture, and the importance of its mission and values. If the new member will serve in a leadership position, then the organization's leadership expectations are also an area that should be given much focus.

Regular One-On-One Meetings

Leaders should meet regularly with direct reports in one-on-one settings. This is to provide feedback on performance, answer questions, encourage them, and more. Part of every agenda at these meetings should be a discussion of the mission, goals, standards, overall performance, and how well the individual is demonstrating the core values. These meetings are especially important for new staff or volunteers who are still learning the basics of the organization and their roles. Early on, new hires don't know what they don't know and need seasoned mentors to help them succeed.

Performance Reviews

As stated above, effective leaders regularly meet with each staff member to build strong relationships and provide feedback on performance. In many organizations, an annual evaluation is provided to each employee that encapsulates their overall performance from the previous year. While good leaders do not wait twelve months before meeting with their staff, the annual evaluation process is necessary to create a record of successes, missteps, and goals as well as to identify candidates for promotion.

These annual meetings between supervisors and those working under their care are perfect times to evaluate, correct, and/or reward team members for not only their work performance but also their demonstration of commitment to the mission and values. Because leaders are holding regular meetings with direct reports throughout the year, there should never be any surprises when the annual evaluation is given. Mistakes and successes must be addressed promptly in order to shape performance of staff, whether new or veterans.

Times of Discipline, Corrective Action, Developmental Plans

Unfortunately, there are times when team members fall short in either their work performance or they violate the core values, and some disciplinary action is needed to correct the issues. The discussions that take place between leaders and the staff are perfect times to reinforce the importance of the mission, work standards, and core values.

When performance problems arise, the leader's first decision is very basic. Does the infraction warrant dismissal? If the answer is yes, then there are established policies that need to be followed legally and ethically to end the person's tenure with the organization. If the person's actions don't lead to dismissal, then a developmental plan is created that addresses the shortcomings, clarifies what needs to change, and identifies a timeline for various actions. The goal of any type of discipline that does not involve dismissal is to address performance problems and restore the person to their original standing within the team.

SUCCESS STORY:
THE POWER
OF DAD

An interview with Brian Pruitt, Founder and CEO of Power of Dad.

Brian Pruitt founded the Power of Dad [POD] organization in 2007, in Saginaw, Michigan. His vision was to combat the epidemic of fatherlessness and improve the quality of relationships between fathers and their children.

Since then, more than fifty volunteers joined the organization, helping to make progress on their mission. Their approach is to bring together trusted mentors and fatherless boys to impart a variety of skills related to success in school, family, and life.

The program launched at a single location and has since expanded to many others, including a Michigan Native American reservation. To date, over 1000 fatherless boys have graduated from the program.

Question: What were your greatest challenges?

Brian: We often struggled with getting enough qualified volunteers. We needed men we could trust and ones that truly loved the kids in the program. They had to be able to overlook bad attitudes and some rebellion, understanding that the boys have never had a father figure in their lives up to that point. Also, we had a hard time raising money for the program. Often, my wife and I had to underwrite the program costs ourselves to keep it running. Fortunately, we did have some area businessmen that helped with costs, and we were able to keep things going.

Question: What are you most proud of?

Brian: I am most proud of the fact that many of the fatherless boys that started with us are now responsible fathers, husbands, and productive citizens in our society. What we did worked!

Question: Was there a time when the team needed to be revised, transformed, or rebuilt? Explain.

Brian: Yes, there came a time when I began to stifle the growth of POD because it was too dependent on my presence, abilities, and passion. So, I changed the model and began to train others to lead. The new train-the-trainer model was our turning point. Instead of being one man with a message, we became many men with a message.

Question: Have you done any training, development, or coaching for your leaders or staff? If so, what did you do and what was the impact?

Brian: Yes, we have done training with our leaders in mentoring, public speaking, facilitating activities, and life coaching. The impact was the confidence of our team grew by leaps and bounds. They felt more equipped to guide the young men that we worked with and to present the curriculum we teach.

Question: What advice do you have for anyone wanting to either launch a new organization or revitalize an existing one?

Brian: Start with the end in mind. In other words, define what success looks like to you. In my case, I wanted to see thousands of fatherless boys become successful despite their early years without father figures in their lives. Also, plan your work and then do it. Layout your mission and values, then set your goals.

Finally, train and trust those around you to take ahold of the vision. This way, your mission will go far beyond what you could do alone, and it will carry on even after you are gone.

CHAPTER 20

RESILIENCY:

ESSENTIAL FOR LONG-TERM SUCCESS

I n the early 1960s, Bob Dylan released a cryptic song entitled "The Times They Are A-Changin'." His lyrics address the often-chaotic period marked by civil rights demonstrations, war protests, political infighting, radical transformation of societal values, and more.

What I find interesting about the song's message is that it is just as relevant today as it was back then. The times are *still* changing, and those changes impact every organization, every team, every family, and every individual on the face of the earth. Many of those changes are retrofitted from the 60s. We still have protests, demonstrations, political infighting, and changing societal values, but a few new ones have shown up in recent years. We can start with a worldwide pandemic, battles over immigration, and a host of other changes. I wonder if Mr. Dylan was amazed when he found out that the marijuana that had to be kept hidden from law enforcement in his early days as an artist, now is readily available at the corner store.

For leaders of organizations, the changes come fast and furious in the form of new government regulations, changing tax code, laws related to employment practices, and a host of others. When hit with unexpected changes, there is an unavoidable breakdown in terms of our sense of well-being, security, and control. In fact, unanticipated change means that we are literally out of control, at least temporarily. For some, the uncertainties cause serious anxiety, nearly paralyzing them until the pace of change slows, which it may never do.

Others, when confronted by chaotic conditions, rise above them, setting a course to regain normalcy in short order. It is likely that on many teams, there is a combination of these paradigms, which only leads to more chaos as the calm individuals wonder what is wrong with the fearful ones and those with greater levels of trepidation wonder why the calm ones cannot grasp the gravity of the situation.

Since the times are going to keep changing, the real question is how can we quickly adjust, maintain team unity, and keep our organizations from being overwhelmed by it all? The answer is found in a single word, *resilience.*

Resiliency Basics

Since your team is subject to ongoing change, disturbances, and adversity, it only makes sense to have a game plan to build resilience in each member of your organization. Here are a few basics to understand in that process.

1.   Organizations, teams, and individuals are in a constant state of change and stress. New challenges appear frequently, often without warning. So, expect them.

2.   Resilience is built *before* adversity, disturbance, unwanted change, or a crisis occurs . . . not during. Preparation is vitally important.

3. Unnecessarily complex systems, inflexibility, strained relationships, and/or the lack of open communication lower a team's ability to bounce back from challenges

4. Immature, unprofessional responses to disruptions such as blaming others, complaining, or attempting to avoid them lower a team's resilience.

5. Professional, mature leaders are essential to an organization's resilience. Without them, change becomes chaos and chaos becomes crisis.

When The Going Gets Tough

So, how do leaders prepare their team members to withstand the stress of adversity, respond correctly, and continue to live the values while pursuing the mission? Here is a strategic approach to this vital initiative:

- Provide ongoing education, training, and coaching so team members understand their roles, job requirements, rules, regulations, and policies.

When the crisis hits, it is no time for any guesswork about any of these factors.

- Regularly revisit the organization's statement of mission. This helps team members remember their purpose and direction.

- Regularly revisit the core values. This helps team members internalize the expected behaviors, regardless of what is happening around them.

- Maintain close contact and open communication between leaders and team members. When conditions become uncertain, we all want assurance from those in authority that contingency plans are in place, and all will be well.

- Provide opportunities for team members to ask questions and receive honest responses from their leaders, even if the response is "I am not sure...but I will find out."

- Ensure that there are supportive relationships within the team. It is easier to endure and overcome challenges if we do not have to do it alone.

- Provide guilt-free access to support services such as counseling, coaching, and a listening ear, using internal and/or external sources.

Leadership in the Midst of the Storm

Over the years, I have worked with leaders during some of their most challenging times, including: world-wide pandemics, the loss of key customers, significant budget cuts, new competitors, and a host of others. In those situations, it became clear that there are certain actions that leaders can take to increase resiliency throughout the team:

Visibility. Even though these leaders were extremely busy during the crises, they made the attempt to be regularly seen by as many staff members as possible. At times, this was simply a brief visit to a particularly busy department or area. At other times, the leader would stop and talk with staff along the way, asking how they were doing and offering encouragement.

I am sad to say that in other companies, those at the top did the exact opposite, seeming to hide in their offices as if waiting for the crisis to pass. The impact on staff from each type of leader was profound. More visible leaders lifted the spirits and reduced the fears of their staff, allowing them to focus on the tasks at hand. Conversely, absent leaders amplified fears and sent shock waves through entire departments.

Strategy, not tactics. When the pressure from a crisis was on, some leaders responded by putting a tighter grip on their operation. Rather than continuing to trust those below them on the organizational chart, the panicked leaders began micromanaging even the smallest tasks.

Naturally, this created resentment from middle managers and supervisors, who ultimately shifted into neutral as their top leaders flailed around in their areas. The much more successful leaders were those who continued to trust those working under their care and instead of spending their time counting widgets…they spent it developing long-term strategies to get out of the quagmire.

Decisiveness. For some leaders, the various crises brought on a sort of analysis-paralysis, whereby they simply stopped making decisions unless they were forced to. Spend money or save? Expand or reduce headcount and inventory?

The reluctance to act covered many areas including personnel. Some organizational leaders failed to dismiss ineffective staff, at any level, even though those individuals were harming the organization's overall performance. Fortunately, other leaders saw the crisis as a time for decisive action and they took charge, hiring necessary personnel, dismissing poor performers, investing in infrastructure, and actually increasing employee compensation as a means of keeping a solid workforce in place.

Contagious faith. Top leaders in every organization set the tone, the tempo, and the culture for the rest of the staff members. I call this being in the 'fishbowl' as employees constantly watch for verbal and nonverbal cues from their leaders about the future. The leaders that refuse to hide but come out and engage their staff with confidence and an uplifting word, leave a wonderful trail of faith about the future. Those that shuffle around, looking defeated, talking about all the problems they face, send unmistakable messages that it's time to seek employment or membership elsewhere. There are very few situations that threaten the existence of an organization. A leader's expressed faith in the future can lift the spirits of the team as they chart a course for success.

After the Storm

Adversity, resistance, challenges, and chaos come in different forms and varying degrees of severity. After a particularly challenging time, it is important for the members of a team to have opportunities to debrief, de-stress, detox, and reset their emotional, mental, and even physical dials.

Just over a year after the COVID pandemic of 2020 hit, I worked with the executives of a large hospital system to design a series of "resiliency" sessions for their nearly 300 leaders, including all executives, directors, managers, and coordinators. We held twelve sessions and invited 20 to 24 leaders to attend each of the two-hour long sessions.

At the start of each session, I welcomed the groups and explained our agenda. Next, one of the top executives greeted the leaders and played a ten-minute PowerPoint and video presentation entitled *Lives Changed, Lessons Learned.*

The presentation covered the impact that the pandemic had on the nation, the community, and the hospital system itself. Inserted into the presentation were some highlights of the previous year, and some unexpected trivia such as top songs of that period, best movies, and so on. I did not include the trivia as filler, but rather to help attendees understand that the pandemic did not stop life from happening. One slide that provided ample proof of that fact showed that the hospital staff had delivered 3000 babies during that same period!

As the executive presented the slides, she also talked about the hospital's excellent response and how many patients were helped during their times of crisis. The presentation concluded with a short video of hospital staff talking about how proud they were of their organization.

Immediately following the slide presentation, the executive shared how the pandemic impacted her personally. Then, we asked the attendees to talk about the impact of COVID on them and their families. Some lost loved ones and there were more than a few tears. This sharing of deep feelings and emotions in the safe setting did much to re-establish a sense of peace and helped heal the emotional wounds.

The final activity was to have each leader identify what she or he learned during the crisis and then recommend any changes that the organization should make to be better prepared and more resilient for any future challenges. These suggestions were written down and later reviewed by the executive team members.

These sessions accomplished much in terms of resiliency and here is why. By design, we had the top leaders of the organization acknowledge the great work done in the PAST as they all dealt with the pandemic. All in attendance were able to talk about how they were impacted and how they felt in the PRESENT. Finally, we had the opportunity to discuss ideas about ways to better handle challenges in the FUTURE. By approaching it this way, we were able to bring the focus back to the mission and core values that never changed, even during a world-wide pandemic.

All we know for certain about adversity, change, and challenges is that they are coming, and we must prepare now for our resiliency to shine when they arrive.

CHAPTER 21

LEAVING YOUR LEGACY

O ne New Year's Day, I noticed an intriguing trend in the advertisements on television. Strangely absent was the endless stream of ads for the necessities of life, such as biscuits, breath mints, and toilet bowl cleaners. In their place was a blitz of commercials designed to capture the attention of thousands of people making resolutions for change in the coming year. The ads promoted weight loss pills, exercise equipment, vitamins, discount fitness centers, and no less than three different products to help people stop smoking. Sponsors knew that these announcements early in

January would generate millions of dollars from an army of people making pledges to change their lifestyles.

I am certain that some individuals seized the moment to become fat-free, smoke-free, and cholesterol-free for the rest of their lives. More power to them. Sadly, I am just as certain that many tried for a short time and then fell back into their old ways. Interestingly, it seems that the advertisers held a similar conviction. In less than a month, the commercials once again featured candy bars and reclining lounge chairs. Why did they change? Because the sponsors knew that by late February, most resolutions were only vague memories and people were ready to return to their more comfortable routines.

Too often, we set goals for positive change when inspired or under stress, only to forget about them when the pressure is off. This is true for individuals and for organizations as well. There is a temptation to back off on commitments made once the initial crisis or motivation wanes. This can happen so subtly.

In business, perhaps one leader begins to mistreat followers, interdepartmental communication shuts down, or one group of employees lets their quality standards slide. Leaders in government may squander time, money, and other resources on projects other than those that support their stated commitments. In the home, parents who made commitments to spend more quality time with their children are tempted to work just a few more hours each week.

You have come too far to allow that to happen.

A New Way of Life

When a person performs a behavior for approximately twenty-eight days in a row, it becomes a habit. This should encourage anyone who has struggled to stay on a new diet or to quit smoking. It is also good news for people involved in organizational change. The principle is the same, although it may take considerably longer than twenty-eight days to transform a nation, business, nonprofit, or family.

The truth is, when something is done consistently over a period, it becomes ingrained. What begins as a novelty, soon becomes a habit, and ultimately transcends into a new way of life. You simply need to take the first step.

A wonderful example of this comes from an organization I worked with in West Virginia. This unionized company of six hundred employees had a long history of labor-management strife. As my staff and I worked with leaders of its management and the union to build a positive culture, we found it difficult to make any real progress. The reason? Everyone was stuck in the past and their legacy was one of division, anger, threats, and failure.

Management kept detailed records of all errors and shop rule violations made by employees. Union workers kept their own unofficial records of management transgressions. In this setting, the most senior people served as tribal elders who kept stories of the other group's misdeeds, real and imagined, alive. Each felt duty bound to warn newly hired employees about the rival tribe, which could never be trusted. Whenever anyone tried to suggest a new way of working together, the ideas were drowned in a flood of negative comments...about the past.

Our organizational assessment survey revealed an amazing truth about historic transgressions. We learned that the worst offenders from either side were no longer even employed there! The stories had taken on lives of their own.

When confronted with this reality, leaders from management and the union began to explore ways of building on their shared future, instead of their fractured past.

After several months of extensive training in leadership and team building, some positive changes began to happen. The corporate culture began to shift some, but there was still a long way to go. To create a new legacy of cooperation and resilience, something big needed to happen... and it did.

In order to accelerate the rate of change, the plant manager initiated a unique program that he called *Clean Slate Day*. Here is how it worked. The manager literally stopped work for several hours and assembled all six hundred employees in a huge, offsite meeting room. Naturally, the managers, wearing white hard hats, sat on one side of the room, and the union members, wearing blue hard hats, sat on the opposite side.

The plant manager walked to the podium and took everyone by surprise when he asked HR staff members to wheel out several huge file cabinets containing complete records of past violations committed by the employees. Amazingly, he announced that as of that moment, he was purging each employee's records of all negative reports. As evidence, he had his HR staff literally empty the files into bins to be later burned!

In an unprecedented move, he graciously gave each employee a completely clean slate regarding disciplinary actions and even poor performance records. This was done without any assurance that the employees would reciprocate in any way.

The plant manager then asked the union employees to give the current managers and supervisors a mental "clean slate" of their past misdeeds as well. In effect, he asked each person to offer and receive forgiveness in order to forge new positive working relationships built on trust and common goals.

Before any of the shocked employees or managers could respond, the plant manager surprised them again. This time, he said that he had purchased six hundred gold-colored hard hats and had them placed by the exit doors. He then extended both a challenge and an exhortation to each one there. He said that everyone that was sincerely ready to forgive the past and embrace a better future was to leave his old blue or white hard hat, and pick up a new gold-colored one upon leaving. He then took off his white hard hat, put on a new gold-colored one, and closed the brief, but life-changing meeting.

At first, no one moved. Then, as if floodgates opened, managers, supervisors, and production employees rose from their seats and headed toward the doors. It did not take long to see the impact of the manager's speech. In fact, the response was overwhelming! When the last employee left the meeting only three gold hard hats remained unclaimed. His plan had worked. Since that time, the organization has grown and prospered as never before. They found a way to break away from the past and release the power of agreement necessary to achieve organizational success. Together, they were able to leave a legacy of success. You can too . . .

Leaving *Your* Legacy

As I shared earlier, we are each here for a purpose and we are here for a limited time. Whether we started life with lots of breaks or struggled each day, we are here now. There is work to be done, lives to be changed, progress to be made, and positive legacies to leave.

Here is the great news: our legacy will not be established by what we did on our worst day, nor by what happened to us on our best day. Instead, we build it one day at a time as we apply our God-given talents to the tasks before us. We will be known and remembered by the sum of our attitudes, behaviors, communications, and decisions. When the work gets hard, show your resiliency, and do not quit . . . your legacy depends on it.

Never give up. Never give in. Always believe.

ABOUT THE AUTHOR

Brian D. Molitor is Chief Executive Officer of Molitor International, an award-winning company with over thirty-five years of experience providing consulting, training, and coaching services to clients in North America, Australia, Europe, the United Kingdom, the Caribbean, and Africa.

Brian's company specializes in organizational development, change management and the creation of customized training programs. Molitor International's own complete line of training materials cover a wide variety of topics including leadership, team building, interpersonal relationships, communication, trust building, conflict resolution, reconciliation, and problem solving.

Over the years, Mr. Molitor has produced and hosted numerous television series on fatherhood, interpersonal relationships, family building, and leadership. These shows have aired worldwide. Brian has served on many executive boards, including area labor–management committees, a statewide prison ministry, and international businesses.

National and international audiences recognize Mr. Molitor as an expert who cuts through the theories of the day and communicates the practical application of foundational principles necessary for organizational and personal success.

He is also a prolific writer of both fiction and non-fiction and his books are enjoyed by readers around the globe. His life has been filled with adventure and travel to faraway places including Australia, Africa, the Caribbean, United Kingdom and more. In his younger days, he worked as a lumberjack, semipro football player, factory laborer, and entrepreneur. When he is not fishing in crocodile-infested waters in the Northern Territories or flying over the tundra in Alaska, he is home with his wife of nearly 40 years in Midland, Michigan. Some of his favorite moments are spent reflecting on his four grown children, five grandchildren, and the grace of God that made it all possible.